Also by The F2

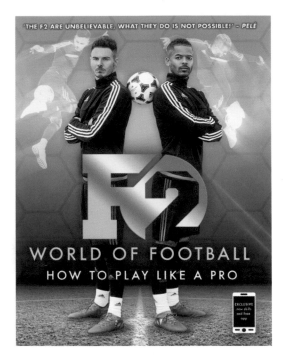

'THE F2 ARE UNBELIEVABLE, WHAT THEY DO IS NOT POSSIBLE!' – PELÉ

WORLD OF FOOTBALL
HOW TO PLAY LIKE A PRO

EXCLUSIVE new skills and free app

TAKE YOUR GAME TO THE NEXT LEVEL

TOP STARS BEST SKILLS

FOOTBALL ACADEMY
HOW TO PLAY LIKE A PRO

NEW FREE APP

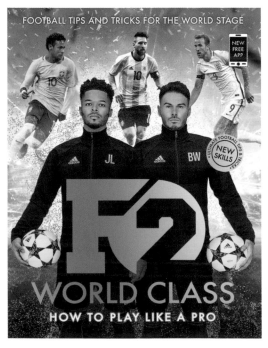

FOOTBALL TIPS AND TRICKS FOR THE WORLD STAGE

NEW FREE APP

ULTIMATE FOOTBALL TIPS & TRICKS
NEW SKILLS

WORLD CLASS
HOW TO PLAY LIKE A PRO

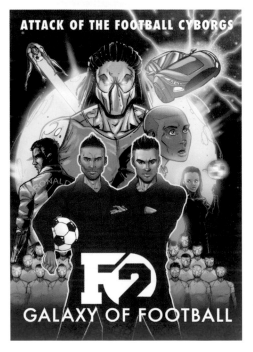

ATTACK OF THE FOOTBALL CYBORGS

GALAXY OF FOOTBALL

ULTIMATE
FOOTBALLER

BLINK
bringing you closer

Published by Blink Publishing
2.25, The Plaza,
535 Kings Road,
Chelsea Harbour,
London, SW10 0SZ

www.blinkpublishing.co.uk

facebook.com/blinkpublishing
twitter.com/blinkpublishing

Flexibind – 978-1-788-702-58-4
Paperback – 978-1-788-703-01-7
Ebook – 978-1-788-702-59-1

A CIP catalogue of this book is available from the British Library.

Design by Steve Leard
Printed and bound in Italy

1 3 5 7 9 10 8 6 4 2

Blink Publishing is an imprint of Bonnier Books UK
www.bonnierbooks.co.uk

To all of our fans and the whole F2 Family.

THE F2 APP

* * *

GET THE ULTIMATE FOOTBALL SKILLS GUIDE FREE ON YOUR SCREEN

Billy: Download our free F2 App and you'll be able to see our skills come to life on your device.

Jez: That's right, we've packed in new, never-before-seen video tutorials and helpful tips so you can learn how to play like a pro. And once you've honed your touch, you can upload your own skill videos and share them with us!

Billy: To access all this exclusive content, download the free app from the iTunes App Store or Google Play Store, launch the app and point your device's camera at the pages with the special phone icon (top right). Then sit back and watch the magic happen!

Jez: It's that simple, so what are you waiting for? Download, read, watch, learn and take your game to the next level. See you on the football pitch!

*The F2 App by The F2 requires an Internet connection to be downloaded and can be used on iPhone, iPad or Android devices. For direct links to download the app and further information, visit www.blinkpublishing.co.uk

Scan this page now for your first video!

CONTENTS

INTRO

Yes guys!

We're back – and this time we truly mean business.

If you love football and tekkers then you've come to the right place because in the pages ahead we're going to pull off the ultimate trick. We are going to build the ultimate footballer, right in front of your eyes.

We'll look into what secret skills and qualities the ultimate footballer needs to have. These will be the bricks that build an absolute baller of a player – the sort of talent who, when he lines up in the tunnel before the match, makes opponents think twice.

Football is a game of opinions and in this book you'll learn plenty of ours as we discuss each attribute the perfect player will need. We'll also dive right in and use our own experiences of meeting these players in real life to pick one for every attribute. You will have your own chance to choose your perfect player. Which of us will you agree with? Or will you choose one we haven't thought of?

There will also be drills and skills to help you learn how to play like the best. Do you want to rainbow flick like Neymar, finish like Kane or scoop it like Messi? We're going to reveal so many hidden secrets. You'll be the envy of your mates when you start pulling off some of these moves.

You can also get up-to-date on what we've been up to since our last book – and there's a lot to catch up on. We've been to the World Cup, launched our own football talent agency and made new videos with a galaxy of stars.

Oh, we almost forgot to say: we've only gone and launched our own football team, F2FC, too! So you'll get the lowdown on that and so much more as we take you Inside The F2. We feel blessed to have the lifestyle we have, and we want to take you behind the scenes.

So it's time to get the ball rolling. Get reading, learning, thinking and practising. If you pay attention you will learn what the ultimate footballer would be capable of.

And who knows? Maybe you'll take yourself one step closer to the elite.

We've had so much fun putting this book together for you, guys. We hope you enjoy reading it just as much.

Love, peace and tekkers,

The F2

OVERVIEW

***

THE RULES OF THE GAME

Billy: Okay, listen up people, building the perfect footballer is serious stuff – particularly because you, the F2 Family, are going to get involved. This isn't the time for mucking about, which is why we've imposed some rules, so we all know where we stand.

So if you're ready, Jez is here to tell you how it's going to work...

Jez: In each chapter, we're going to go through the top 11 attributes that the Ultimate Footballer will need: the skills requiredd for the perfect player.

Both of us will have our say on each of these attributes. We'll discuss why

THE SKILLS

Passing
Speed
Mentality
Tekkers
Volleys
Dribbling
Finishing
Free-kicks
Heading
Tackling
Engine

they are important to the game and which players have them in their locker.

Billy: And there's more – we'll also teach you how you can develop the attribute yourself with tips from us and from the stars themselves.Then we're going to put it all on the line. Jez and I will both choose a player for each of the attributes. The guy we think is the best example, the top man, for that skill. One-by-one, we'll give a shout-out to our favourite footballer in each field. And here's the important bit, so I'm going to underline it, to really make the point: **each player can only be picked once.**

Jez: So, if, say Billy chooses Lionel Messi for dribbling, then no one else can select Messi at all for anything. He's taken him right off the table in one sneaky move. Pure filth right there from Wingrove!

Billy: I'm getting absolutely slaughtered, here! But the same goes for Jez. If he chooses Luka Modrić for passing then that's that – there's no chance for either of us to select the Croatian playmaker for any other category. It's going to be an amazing roll call.

Jez: And this is where things will get feisty because neither of us is about to back down and say that we picked the wrong guy. It's an F2 face-off and it's always going to be highly charged. Expect it to get a bit messy!

After that heated debate you will know our favourite players and then we will turn the tables and ask you to select yours. Which of us chose the better players? You get to decide and let us know. Who would you pick for your dream player?

Billy: Mate, can you imagine for a moment how awesome the ultimate footballer would be? A single player with top, top ability in every single one of those categories – the guy would be a world-beater. And he'd have to be. Imagine if we were playing Mars at football and we needed a player capable of taking on the Martians. That's the sort of talent we are aiming for – interplanetary genius.

Jez: Well listen, if we're going to go on a science-fiction vibe then a good way of understanding what this book is all about is to imagine we're building a footballing Frankenstein's monster together. We've got a big table in a lab and we're stitching together feet here, a heart there and a brain on top, until we have the kind of being who will scare opponents, just like Frankenstein's monster.

Billy: You know what? There's a decent lesson to be learned in the fact that we need to take different qualities from different players: it's because even at the highest level, real football is a team game. Players like Cristiano Ronaldo and Lionel Messi are unreal talents, but even the top stars have a weakness here and there.

You wouldn't rely on Messi to defend any more than you would depend on Virgil van Dijk to do a pitch-length mazy dribble. Harry Kane is one of the greatest finishers we've ever seen, but Kevin De Bruyne's your man when it comes to passing.

Jez: Exactly, and just like all the best teams are made up of the best players, our ultimate footballer is composed of the different parts of the best players. We're only interested in the strengths here, we leave everything else behind until we're left with an actual fantasy footballer – the stuff of dreams.

Billy: Dreams is the right word, Jez. It's the ultimate dream – to build the perfect footballer. It's going to be feisty and fun, so let's get on with it.

PASSING

* * *

CHAPTER 1

PASSING

Billy: You know Jez, it sounds funny to say this, but in the old days passing wasn't actually as important in football as it is now. For a long time, English football was more about a 'kick and rush' style. A defender or goalkeeper would hoof a long, hopeful ball up the field and the teams would pile forward to try and get to it first.

Jez: Hmmm, I've got to say, I'm glad those days have gone. I think it's much more fun to watch matches between teams that believe in strong vision and precise passing. That's what I call the beautiful game. So that's why we had to have passing as one of the qualities of our ultimate footballer. He's going to be a player for the modern game – and a man for the future, not the past.

Billy: Yes, how times have changed! Teams like Real Madrid and PSG are now off the charts with their passing accuracy. In the Premier League, you can't look further than Man City. They absolutely smashed it with possession when they won the 2019 title.

Historically, other teams have been the pass wizards. Arsenal at their peak under Arsène Wenger pinged that ball around perfectly.

Jez: When I think of passing accuracy and individuals, I keep coming back to Luka Modrić. He has averaged up to 90% passing accuracy for Real. To pull off numbers like that in La Liga is unreal. Other star names might have got more attention, but it was Modrić's passes that made them tick.

Lionel Messi, Paul Pogba and Toni Kroos are also players who are handy with the passing. Take Messi – his passing isn't actually the first thing you think about when you imagine him at his best. You're more likely to picture him dribbling or remember one of his amazing goals. But that guy can pick out a pass.

Billy: He really can, and when you think about how heavily marked he is, the fact he can thread so many inch-perfect passes is even more impressive. David Silva is really good at passing, too. When I picture him, it's that left foot of his pinging pin-perfect passes to his teammates I remember.

Jez: Hold on, hold on... 'Pinging pin-perfect passes?' What's with all the words beginning with 'P', Bill?

Billy: I'm a poet and you know it.

Jez: Erm, okay... getting back to it, do you remember that pass Kevin

19

De Bruyne made against Stoke? He ignored all the easy options around him and threaded a ball through a load of players for Leroy Sané's goal. Unbelievable vision and accuracy!

Billy: That's right, vision is important because accurate passing isn't just about what you do with your feet but what you do with your eyes. You have to be able to see the pass before you make it. Take someone like Mesut Özil – vision is a big part. In fact, many of

his teammates and coaches over the years have used the word 'vision' to praise him.

Jez: We filmed with Steven Gerrard and his passing was better than most of the players we've worked with. The way he catches the ball is just so sweet. He's got a range of passes in his locker: he can nail a five-yard or 40-yard pass. He knows how to put the perfect weight and power on the ball.

'DO YOU REMEMBER THAT PASS KEVIN DE BRUYNE MADE AGAINST STOKE?'

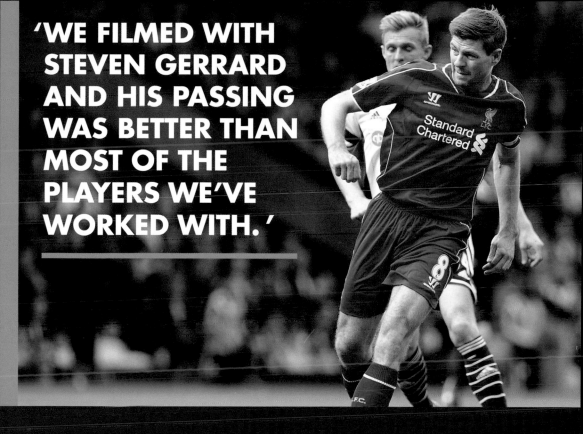

'WE FILMED WITH STEVEN GERRARD AND HIS PASSING WAS BETTER THAN MOST OF THE PLAYERS WE'VE WORKED WITH. '

Billy: Yes, guys like him know that making sure the ball lands on the correct foot of their teammate is important. You need to be able to get it to their strong foot or make it land on the head of the player, if that's where he wants it. And yes, you should be aiming to do it first time. This is what we want for our ultimate player.

Another good thing about passing is that you can use it to exhaust your opposition in the opening half of a game. Mikel Arteta, assistant coach at Man City, says that if you ping the ball around for 20 minutes or so you can have the opponents chasing round after the ball so much that they get worn down physically. Then they will start making mistakes, which you can capitalise on.

Jez: Okay, so let's wind this up now. But before we go, I want to remember something one of the greatest players of all time said. Johan Cruyff was an absolute legend for the Dutch national team back in the day. He said the measure of a good pass is not the pass itself, but the next pass.

So, when you pass the ball to someone, it's their next pass which really shows how well you did with yours. It's like their pass is a tribute to your pass. I think once you understand that, you understand passing.

✱ ✱ ✱

PASSING

BILLY:
KEVIN DE BRUYNE

8	SPEED
10	VISION
9	TOUCH
9	FINISHING
9	TEKKERS

Billy: Now this face-off is an absolute beauty. Both these guys can spray the passes around like few others in the game right now. I'm going to kick this off by asking if you can imagine them both in the same team? The stats! Their team would have 100% possession!

Jez: Yeah, it would be unreal. Modrić is an immense talent – he's one of the most assured and intelligent players I've ever seen. How many times have we seen him pick up the ball from defence and just effortlessly move it up to the attackers? It's like the guy is skating on ice – but he makes it look so easy!

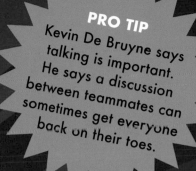

PRO TIP
Kevin De Bruyne says talking is important. He says a discussion between teammates can sometimes get everyone back on their toes.

JEZ:
LUKA MODRIĆ

SPEED	7
VISION	10
TOUCH	10
FINISHING	8
TEKKERS	10

Billy: Not only that, he can do it when it matters. He has that big-match nerve that's so rare but so, so valuable. But let's talk about my man De Bruyne. Jamie Redknapp said he reckons this guy is the best passer of the ball he's ever seen.

The thing about Kevin is that he is great at a whole load of passes. You can't name me a single type of pass he isn't brilliant at. He's just got so much class and smarts. No wonder he's so prized.

Jez: I'm going to call it: Modrić is the winner here because his long-range passing is that bit better than De Bruyne's. That bit better than anyone's, to be fair!

ÖZIL BOUNCE PASS

Origin: **Mesut Özil, Germany, 2010s**
Skill type: **Pass**
Difficulty rating: **8**
Tekkers rating: **9**
Frequently used by: **Mesut Özil**

Jez: The German wizard was at his magical best when he pulled this baby out of the bag against Denmark. Some people thought for a moment that he'd scuffed the pass but Özil is a player who always surprises. Knocking the pass into the ground first meant he could bounce it over his opponent's outstretched leg. With that one pass he took two defenders out of the game in an instant. Or, like Özil, you can also use it to beat the keeper in a one-on-one. Now, that's tekkers!

Make sure your weight is over the ball

Chop down on the back of the ball at an angle

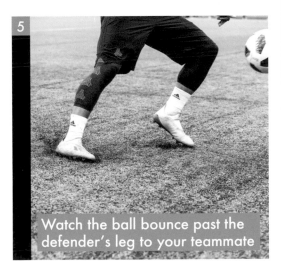

Watch the ball bounce past the defender's leg to your teammate

* * *

PASSING DRILL
THROUGH BALLS

There's no better sight in football than an attacker running onto a perfectly weighted through-ball and smashing it in top bins. Well, the beginning of that is the through-ball itself. So, if you want to roll those beauties in like Mesut Özil or David Luiz, you can start by working with this drill. It really improves your attacking movement in the final third. Your passing ability and the weight of your passes are also taken to a whole new level. Yes guys!

Instructions

1. Set up three cones or mannequins on the pitch. These will be your 'opponents'.

2. Player A stands by the 'opponents' and passes the ball to Player B, as they approach the area.

3. Player B pings it back to Player A.

4. Player A then passes it past the 'opponents' as Player B runs through them.

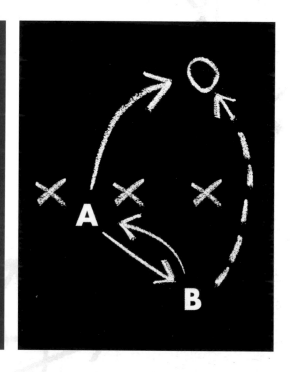

PRO TIP
Do the same drill but with different passing forms, like clips and chips, to make it trickier.

INSIDE THE F2

***

THE WORLD CUP FINALS

Billy: Jez, I think it's fair to say we will never forget our time in Russia.

Jez: It's so true. You have to go to the World Cup to realise how wild it is. Fans from all around the world are there to watch the greatest ballers on the planet compete for the game's ultimate prize. We had goose pimples watching those games.

And every time we saw an England fan in the Three Lions shirt, we were pumped. It's just an awesome feeling to be over there, supporting the guys. When you're in the stadium at a World Cup match and someone scores, the atmosphere is electric.

Billy: That's right, Jez. You know the entire planet is tuned into these matches on TV. You feel like you're in the centre of the footballing universe and there's a reason for that: it's because you are.

We liked Russia. Sometimes people in the media say negative things about Russia but our experience of the country was really positive. We've no complaints but a heap of happy memories.

Jez: We didn't spend too much time in Russia because we didn't want to be away from our families for a whole month, so we flew in and out for the matches. That made it really special because it meant we got the buzz of what it was like back in England, where everyone was getting excited, then flying out to watch the games, then coming back to feel the buzz in England again. We got the best of both worlds, we really did.

Billy: And the excitement over here really built, didn't it? Every time we got back to England we sensed more and more people believed they could go all the way and win the tournament. Everyone was giving it: "Football's coming home!" But we weren't quite so convinced...

Jez: Yeah, I was actually surprised England got as far as they did. Somehow we ended up in the semi-final of the World Cup. That's the best England have done since... forever. Well, since 1990 anyway. But I wasn't getting caught up in the expectation.

Billy: Yep, same. I mean, listen, I'm a Spurs fan and I see England the same way I see Spurs – even when they're on an amazing run and look like they're going to win something, you have to assume something is going to go wrong.

I think when you look at England over the years, you'd have to admit the chances of them pulling off something like a World Cup win are pretty slim. But it was nice to see young players out there performing with so much confidence. They were fearless.

So, I didn't get carried away, I didn't think we'd win the World Cup. I wasn't singing about football coming home. But the signs for the future of the England team are bright.

Jez: What are you thinking about Gareth Southgate, Bill?

Billy: Well, he's settled in and I think his man-management is good. He has taken over a good generation and they seem to be responding to it.

Jez: There are reasons to get optimistic with England, but I personally try to avoid getting carried away. You know what they say: it's the hope that kills you. I think we should just enjoy watching these

young England players and see what Southgate can do with them. If we put too much pressure on, it might mess things up.

But who knows, maybe one day England will get to a final. That would be amazing! For us, the best part of the 2018 tournament was being able to go to the final and watch France win it. That's a privilege and we know how lucky we are. Tickets are so hard to get hold of, but we're in the fortunate position of being able to go as part of our jobs.

It was good to be there and I remember Paul Pogba played really well as France beat Croatia 4-2.

Billy: Yeah, France v Croatia was not a final many people would have predicted. But international football can throw up these surprises. We loved being there and what a moment for Didier Deschamps, winning it as a coach 20 years after he won it as France's captain. I love how football throws up stuff like that.

Jez: It's true. We loved being there as history is made in these tournaments. Hopefully we'll go to loads of major tournaments in the future. But hats off to Russia, they surprised a lot of people with how they hosted the World Cup.

SPEED

CHAPTER 2

* * *

SPEED

Jez: There's no two ways about it: speed is a massive part of the modern game. For many players, but particularly wingers, attacking midfielders and full-backs, it's absolutely vital. To be honest, footballers are now athletes, they really, really are. So if you've got speed, you've got a good chance at making it.

Billy: That's right. Choosing this attribute for our ultimate footballer really was a no-brainer: speed is important because, at the most basic level, if your opponent can't keep up with you then you've immediately got the edge on them. It's that simple, isn't it?

Jez: And that's why players who can run fast with the ball at their feet move for such high transfer fees. But listen, it's not just being fast with the ball that matters. Being fast without the ball is also a big deal. Look at the teams that are strong on the counter-attack – their players have to be super-pacy. Speedy wingers and fast-sprinting forwards will always have the edge on the back line.

Billy: That's true, Jez, and you also need to be fast if you're a defender. How else are you going to keep up with those fast attackers unless you're all about the pace yourself?

Jez: Once you drill down into it, you discover there are really two types of speed: acceleration and top speed. Acceleration is important because it's how quickly you can get away from your opponent. Thierry Henry had exceptional acceleration over five to 10 yards.

More recently, you can look at Sadio Mané and Mo Salah. They are both exceptional over five, 10, 15 yards. You can't leave out Raheem Sterling, either. His acceleration is unreal. Acceleration is really important because once you've passed a player, you can get away!

Billy: And the second type, top speed, is also important. You've got players who are fantastic at top-end speed, like Gareth Bale. They can push the ball into space and get after it. Did you know Usain Bolt called Bale the 'fastest footballer in the world'? I mean, when the fastest man in the world is praising your pace, you know you've absolutely smashed it.

Jez: And it's funny you mention Bolt, because they reckon one of Kylian Mbappé's sprints against Monaco was actually faster than Bolt! Kylian has got up to 38kph, which is faster than when Bolt set

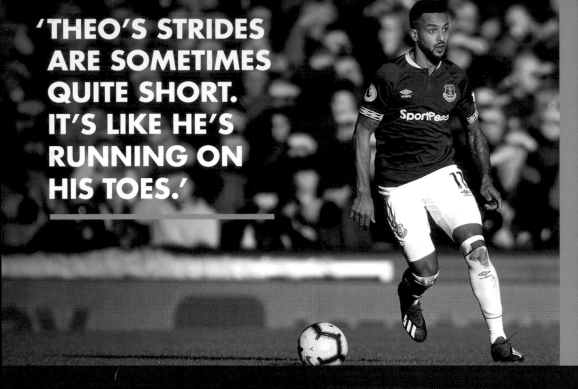

'THEO'S STRIDES ARE SOMETIMES QUITE SHORT. IT'S LIKE HE'S RUNNING ON HIS TOES.'

the world record for 100m. And if we're talking stats, then Leroy Sané has reached 35kph, so he's got to be right in the mix, too.

And you know what? Even though we talk a lot about speed in reference to attackers, defenders need it too. Van Dijk has a massive stride but he's deceptively quick. He can make the ground up. Kyle Walker's pace is dangerous in attack but also effective in defence.

I've got to say, Bill, you're the fastest out of us two. Your acceleration is exceptional – you're so quick over five to 15 yards.

Billy: Thanks, mate. But I'm not perfect. I raced against a 200m hurdler once. He said: 'You're rapid

but your technique is awful.' Even though I beat him by a fair few metres, he gave me some great advice.

He told me my legs cross over as I run, I don't run straight and I don't drive with my quads. You too can find out what you're doing wrong and how to improve.

Jez: So the big question is, how do you get to your fastest speed? What can you do to get faster on the field? Theo Walcott has been one of the fastest players of the Premier League era so I reckon he's worth listening to on this.

Theo reckons if you want to run fast on the pitch, you should start low. And if you picture his runs in your mind, you'll see how he does this – when he sets off on a run his head is down, and it's only after 15 yards that he straightens up his posture.

Theo's strides are sometimes quite short. It's like he's running on his toes. But then there's Gareth Bale's technique – he really opens his legs out for big strides. But physically they are different guys, so you should look at these two versions and see which one works best for you.

Billy: The bottom line is that players are getting faster every year. It's just incredible.

When Premier League academies line up trialists, the first thing they look at is their speed. The experts feel you can work on things like passing, dribbling and so on. But speed and stamina are so important that they look for those first.

If you want to improve your speed, YouTube is a great place to learn. If you type in, 'How to improve my speed' you'll get good advice. There are a load of videos with all the details on how your body should be and how to use your arms in the right way.

Jez: It's really worth working on your speed. The average Premier League footballer covers nearly 12 kilometres over 90 minutes, but that isn't one long run, it's made up of bursts. If you work on your pace, you're going to feel the benefit quickly.

And by adding speed to our ultimate footballer, we're going to feel the benefit too. He'll skin his opponents!

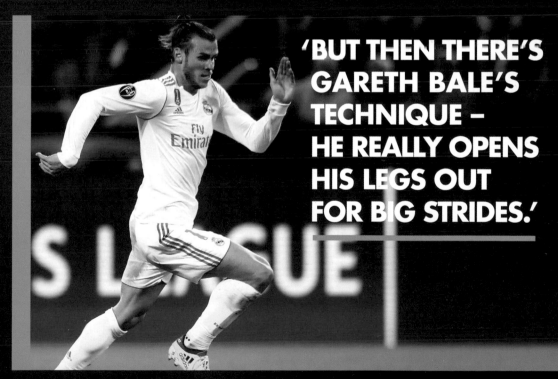

'BUT THEN THERE'S GARETH BALE'S TECHNIQUE – HE REALLY OPENS HIS LEGS OUT FOR BIG STRIDES.'

* * *

SPEED

BILLY:
KYLIAN MBAPPÉ

10	SPEED
8	VISION
8	TOUCH
8	FINISHING
9	TEKKERS

Billy: Come on, Jez. Just be honest: there's absolutely no argument here. Aubameyang is an incredible player and an amazing character – I absolutely love the guy. But when it comes to speed, he's not going to be faster than Mbappé, is he?

Jez: I'm not so sure, you know. I reckon my man Aubameyang could give him a run for his money if they went head-to-head.

Billy: And my oh my, wouldn't that be a race worth watching? But Mbappé is still my man for speed. He managed 10.55 metres per second when he scored against his old team Monaco.

Jez: Well, if we're going to talk stats then you should know that Aubameyang got up to 35kph during his first season with the Gooners.

JEZ:
PIERRE-EMERICK AUBAMEYANG

SPEED	9
VISION	7
TOUCH	8
FINISHING	8
TEKKERS	9

Billy: Mate, you can chuck as many stats around as you like – Mbappé's going to edge this one. You know it!

Jez: Hmmm. Maybe, but you've got to remember he's 10 years younger than Aubameyang. Who would win a race between the two of them in their prime? I think you know the answer.

Billy: It'd be close, that's for sure. I'm going to say Auba's big skill is the ability to maintain his balance and strength at the highest speed. Mbappé, on the other hand, has explosive acceleration. Like we said earlier, there are different types of speed. And these guys have got them covered between them.

GET THE DRILLS

* * *

SPEED DRILL
LIGHT GATES

Yes guys! So, you want to become rapid like Kylian Mbappé? Or get a top speed like Sadio Mané? Here's a drill to maximise your explosive pace. The first step is to find out how fast you are already, and then you can measure the benefits of your work. This is what all the top pros do. They work with light gates, which are digital sensors used for timing. If you have access to them, they are great for timing your acceleration and top speed. You'll discover how fast you can get from standing still to max pace, and what exactly your top speed is.

Instructions

1. Place one light gate at 10 metres from your starting point.

2. Place another one at 30 metres.

3. Race from your start point through the gates at maximum effort.

4. Repeat to measure improvement.

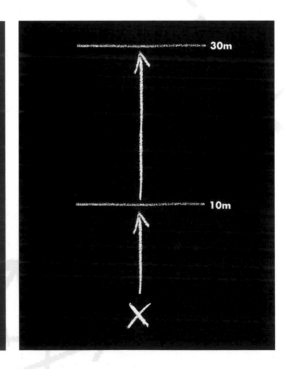

▼ Equipment
Two sets of light gates.
(Or some cones and a stop watch).

PRO TIP
If you don't have access to light gates, you can use cones – just put a mate on each of the cones with a timer, and off you go.

▼ Equipment

Sports power chute. (Sports power chutes aren't expensive, but if you don't have one, then you can get a teammate to put their hands round your waist or chest from behind. Or they can hold your t-shirt. This will give a similar drag to a parachute!)

PRO TIP
Want to mix things up a bit? Then try using different sized parachutes/different friends to get the most out of this drill.

GET THE DRILLS

* * *

SPEED DRILL
PARACHUTE RUN

Here's another brilliant way to up your speed. The benefit of this drill is that it builds your power – particularly your explosive power, and it's explosive power that players like Gareth Bale have. Once you start working on this, you'll see the results in games when you leave your opponent eating your dust. The drill will provide resistance, meaning your power builds even more.

Instructions

1. Make sure you have space all around for you this one – this is best done in a large sports hall or, better yet, outside.

2. Follow the instructions to correctly put the parachute on.

3. Start running! You'll feel the drag from the chute trying to slow you down.

4. Each time you do this one, you can up the distance/time you run for to keep improving your pace.

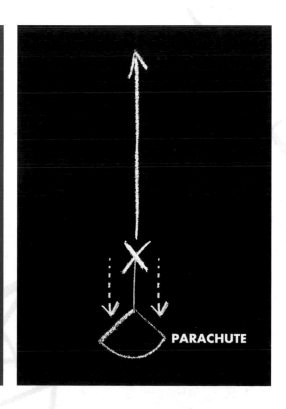

PARACHUTE

MENTALITY

CHAPTER 3

BILLY VS JEZZA

MENTALITY

Jez: Listen up, in modern-day football I think this one is the key. It's the hardest attribute to scout and pick up but in many ways the most important. That's why the FA is now very big on the psychological side of the game.

In the old days, it was always players like Roy Keane, Patrick Vieira and John Terry that were mentioned as mentally strong players, but don't think it's just some players in a team who need to be mentally strong.

It's not just centre-backs or centre-midfielders who need this quality. The fact is that you need it in all positions and that includes the creative ones. Cristiano Ronaldo and Lionel Messi are both strong psychologically.

Billy: Precisely, Jez. Look at that: the two biggest players in the world are really big on this topic. They've even talked about how important it is to get the right mentality. Ronaldo said mental strength is 'just as important as physical strength and it helps me to achieve more on and off the pitch.' He says that listening to the right music before a match helps motivate him.

Jez: Yeah, and when Messi spoke about success, he said: 'For me it's all about having the courage to get up and try again.' And he even explained why he has that courage – he said it's through his 'love for the game.'

There are so many players who have a strong mentality. Andrea Pirlo, for instance, was one of the most composed players I've ever seen. He wasn't just physically composed but mentally too. That's no coincidence – I don't think you can really have one without the other.

Billy: I always think back to David Beckham's mental strength after what he went through. In 1998 he got sent off in the World Cup and faced huge abuse and even threats. People were properly nasty to him, but he bounced back and won everyone over. That's incredible mentality right there.

It really is vital because you can't win trophies without having players in your side who have the right mentality and leadership skills. If you have four or five of them in your team, then you'll win trophies. It's as simple as that.

Jez: Yeah, look at Chelsea when they were winning titles. They had Michael Ballack, Didier Drogba, Frank Lampard, John Terry and Claude Makélélé. Those guys were mentally strong and really big on leadership.

They were winners. The type that get you through to finals and win you finals. The sort of guys who get you to the last hurdle in the league and push you over it.

Billy: The reality of football is that you are going to have good days and bad. That's just football, that's just life. But when you have a bad day, it's really important that you have the right mentality to overcome the setbacks and still succeed. It's like what Thiago Silva said after 10-man PSG beat Chelsea: it was because they were 'sturdy' and had mental strength.

Goalkeepers need this attribute more than anyone because their mistakes are so game-changing. They can get pelted when they make a mistake.

David de Gea has dropped some clangers on the biggest stages but has continued to believe in himself and overcome them. Manuel Neuer said he is successful because 'I don't feel the fear. I'm always thinking positive.'

Jez: You know, I feel like we need to mention Steven Gerrard again here. He overcame so many setbacks early

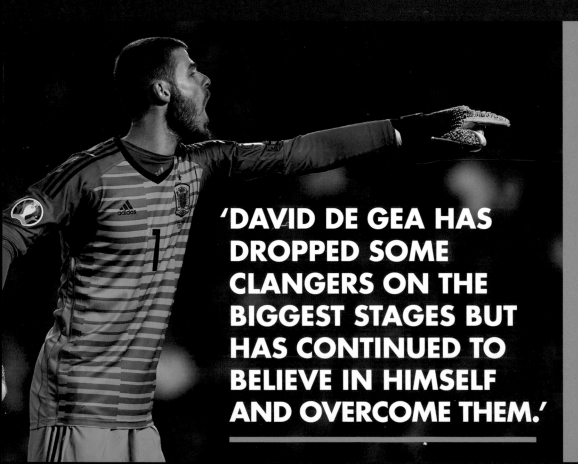

'DAVID DE GEA HAS DROPPED SOME CLANGERS ON THE BIGGEST STAGES BUT HAS CONTINUED TO BELIEVE IN HIMSELF AND OVERCOME THEM.'

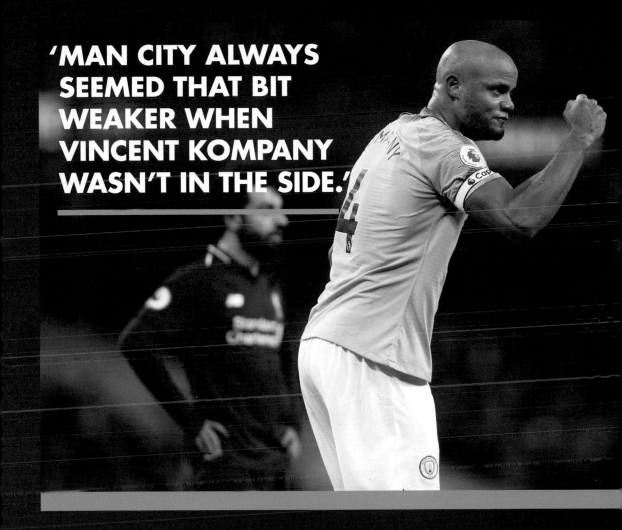

'MAN CITY ALWAYS SEEMED THAT BIT WEAKER WHEN VINCENT KOMPANY WASN'T IN THE SIDE.'

in his career and became a mentally tough player. You can literally measure his strength by how many big games he scored in: the Champions League final, a Uefa Cup final, an FA Cup final and a League Cup final.

And sometimes you notice how mentally strong a player is when he isn't playing. Man City always seemed that bit weaker when Vincent Kompany wasn't in the side. He's just got such a fearless presence and he's developed good leadership skills, which are vital.

Billy: A tip from the top: Gary Neville says that a strong mentality is definitely something you can build on if you're not really feeling it already. He said a part of it is to surround yourself with the right people.

And remember, at the end of the day, it's all about winning. So even when you're playing with your mates you have to focus on football, not friendship. You have plenty of time to be friends off the pitch, but when you're playing, you have to want to win.

MENTALITY

8	SPEED
9	VISION
9	TOUCH
9	FINISHING
10	TEKKERS

BILLY:
CRISTIANO RONALDO

Jez: There's a reason why, since Stevie G took over at Ibrox, everyone says Rangers' mentality has improved. It's because that guy is so mentally tough it's almost unreal. As a new gaffer he's transferring one of the big strengths of his playing days to his players.

Billy: I hear you Jez, and I agree. He's a tough nut, is Stevie. When you look at all the setbacks he overcame, his mentality must be spot-on to keep his eyes on the prize.

But come on, if we're talking mentality then no player in the history of the game is as strong as Cristiano Ronaldo. His mind is like a sledgehammer.

Look at every player and manager he has played with or for – they have all talked about how strong he is.

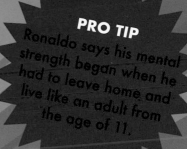
SPEED	8
VISION	9
TOUCH	7
FINISHING	9
TEKKERS	7

JEZ:

STEVEN GERRARD

Jez: I know, but I'm sticking with my guy. In the 2005 Champions League final, with his Liverpool team 3-0 down at half-time, he stayed strong. He gave a half-time team talk that turned it round. Then he went out on the pitch and got the first goal of the comeback. That's historic stuff, and you won't find a stronger single example of mental strength.

Billy: Yeah, but Sir Alex Ferguson said that Ronaldo is one of the most courageous players he has ever managed. And coming from a tough gaffer like him, I think that's big praise.

Jez: You know what? I'm just glad to have seen these players in their prime and to have met them both. Either would be a great example to our Ultimate Footballer.

PANENKA

done

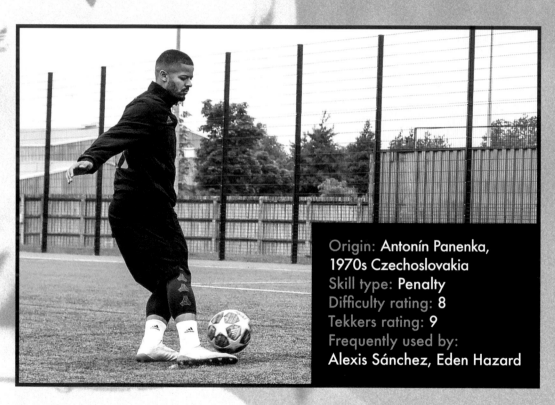

Origin: **Antonín Panenka,
1970s Czechoslovakia**
Skill type: **Penalty**
Difficulty rating: **8**
Tekkers rating: **9**
Frequently used by:
Alexis Sánchez, Eden Hazard

Jez: The big thing with the Panenka is the element of surprise. Most times, a goalkeeper will choose a side at a penalty, which means if all goes well you can chip the ball into the empty middle of the goal. The keeper will have dived one way or another and they'll have no chance to recover and save the ball. But know that this is high-risk tekkers. You'll have to be calm and collected to pull it off, so only attempt it if you've got that ice in your veins.

1

Short run up

2

Fake as if to strike through the ball

3

At the last second, chip the ball

4

No follow-through

5

Top bins!

'YOU'LL HAVE TO BE CALM AND COLLECTED TO PULL IT OFF.'

1 Short run up

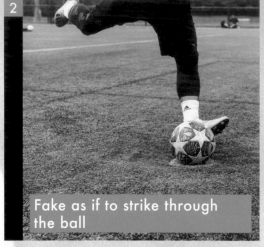

2 Fake as if to strike through the ball

3 At the last second, chip, no follow-through

Feeling confident?

Try the no-look Panenka!

It's all in the eyes

* * *

BILLY'S INJURY

Billy: I've talked about my injuries in some of our previous books and there's more news on that front. I've had injuries to my knee and my Achilles tendon and I have to admit, it's been a really tough experience.

Jez: Yeah man, it's been hard watching you suffer so much. But you've been an absolute legend in how you've dealt with it. You've been so strong.

Billy: Thanks, Jez. It's not always been easy, though. The thing is, people, everything in the human body is connected. So as soon as something goes wrong with my hip, my knee will take the brunt of it. So then my knee goes, and because my knee has gone I am running differently and then my Achilles goes.

Jez: It's a cycle.

Billy: So you have to strengthen the right areas. This is something I've been focusing on, but to this day I know I can probably work on it even more, to make sure I strengthen in the right way.

But at the same time, I can't just give up making content for The F2 because there's a lot of pressure on me. I've been told so many times: Bill,

if you want to be injury-free you have to sacrifice something. Whether it's content for our YouTube channel or playing games – something has to go.

But that's easier said than done. I just haven't listened properly to the advice. I know that sounds bad, but when you're having to juggle creating content for your fans so that they are engaged, you don't want to lose the momentum on what you've worked on for years and years. Not only that: we've got a channel to run and other business too, so there's this underlying pressure for me to carry on working and get fit without resting properly.

Jez: That pressure can feel the same whether it's one of us creating content for The F2, or it's a top star playing in the Champions League who needs to keep their place and provide for their family.

Billy: Exactly. And that's what so many of my injuries have stemmed from: coming back too early and getting into action before my body was ready. And I suppose I got to the point where my body just said to me: you're simply doing far too much.

It's really tough trying to find time to get proper rehab, rest and then film. There's so much to balance. You can't have both.

Jez: What do you think will happen for you in the future with all this, my man?

Billy: I feel like I'll try to rest a bit more. It is the playing that does it. But it's good to get back on the pitch and kick a ball. That always feels great. So maybe the injury is something I might have to live with, knowing my tendonitis might just have to be managed. The burning sensation is still there.

Jez: What about for people reading this – what advice would you have on dealing with injuries? I mean, we've all had them…

Billy: My advice to younger people is actually quite simple: don't get into the position I'm in! All of my injuries could have been avoided if I'd done the right things when I was younger: if I'd stretched, if I'd always eaten the right food before and after matches.

I should have prioritised recovery rather than playing back-to-back matches every day of the week. I've done that for years and it's more football than the body can take. And all the time I wasn't eating properly, I wasn't stretching properly and I wasn't resting properly.

It's as simple as this: if I'd done the right things when I was younger, I'd be in a better place now. I'd be able to cope with the strain. Don't wait until you get the injury to make the change. Make the change now. Prevention is better than cure. Most people wait, but you should do it from the start. And the best change you can make right now is to stretch more. I feel most people in the UK don't do enough stretching. I went to Canada and kids there spend two hours stretching in the morning, they do yoga. They're so supple – they can do backflips!

Jez: Prevention rather than cure is good advice. But you shouldn't be too hard on yourself, Billy. The F2 Family loves you and we don't want you getting more injuries. Take care of yourself, mate.

Billy: Beautiful words, I'm filling up here…

Jez: Ha! Dry your eyes, mate. But it's true that there's a lot involved in keeping The F2 moving and expanding. We work pretty relentlessly. People might say, 'You can't count what you do as work' but it is. If you were in our shoes for a day, you'd see that.

Obviously, I'm fully grateful for our position and the opportunities we've had. I think we've got the best job in the world. But the truth is we work extremely hard. We're running about five businesses. People only see the tip of the iceberg, but 90% of it is invisible: negotiations, planning, strategising. It's relentless. The amount of WhatsApp groups and email chains we're in is unreal…

On top of that we need to film the videos. We're both so grateful for where we are but seriously, it takes a lot of hard work!

'I SHOULD HAVE PRIORITISED RECOVERY, RATHER THAN PLAYING BACK-TO-BACK MATCHES EVERY DAY OF THE WEEK.'

TEKKERS

CHAPTER 4

BILLY VS JEZZA

★ ★ ★

TEKKERS

Billy: Tekkers is a big deal for The F2 but also an attribute that is frequently misunderstood by fans. You see, tekkers is about more than entertaining the crowd. It's not just about flash tricks or self-indulgent skills. It's an important part of the game and is so much more than being flash.

Jez: Oh, so much more. Tekkers is only tekkers if it helps the team do well. It's got to be about the team and about winning, not just about one player showing off.

Billy: Exactly, Jez. Tekkers is your ID. It's who you are as a player. And when you look at the best players down the years, their technique is simply just better than anyone else's. Look at my favourite, Ronaldinho: his technique is probably better than almost anyone in history.

Jez: Having ultimate tekkers is being the most entertaining and fluid footballer, with the most flair. It's the difference between just scoring a free kick and getting it top bins. It's about that extra bit of quality. It's finding a whole new level.

Billy: Some people can kind of control the ball – but some people can really control the ball and do it in their stride. Dele Alli is a good example of that. He has exceptional receiving skills. He can receive it on his chest, heel, thigh or foot. Or over his shoulder. That's tekkers right there.

When you can receive a cross-field ball that has travelled 50 yards to you and stop it dead, that's tekkers. To kill the ball dead is just that next level up. Then again, being able to deliver that pass in the first place and put it on a button is tekkers. When a ball like that just slices through the air, that's beautiful football.

The standard of football is being raised all the time and it makes the game better to watch. I feel blessed to be alive at this moment in time, when football is getting more and more entertaining. I feel blessed to be here at a time when technique is becoming more important and more intricate.

Jez: Neymar is an obvious current example of a player with top-class tekkers. To me, he's like Ronaldinho in his level of tekkers and the variety of skills he has in his locker. I know he's also been compared to Pelé and, when you're being mentioned in the same breath as those two rock stars, you just know your tekkers is off the scale.

Billy: It's true. Pelé himself is a fan of Neymar's tekkers. He said he is better

'TO BE THE BEST EVER, MESSI MUST FIRST BECOME BETTER THAN NEYMAR.'

— PELÉ

than Messi! He said: 'To be the best ever, Messi must first become better than Neymar.' Imagine having that said about you!

Paul Pogba and Eden Hazard are also well worth watching if you want to see some players who are up there with their tekkers. Plus, Cristiano Ronaldo and Lionel Messi, of course.

On their day, Mesut Özil and Alexis Sánchez are in this category too. I recommend that you watch the highlights compilations of all these players on YouTube. You'll see a great show and you can learn from them. You'll get a tekkers masterclass.

Jez: Probably the best of all time at tekkers was Zinedine Zidane. His technique was incredible. He had amazing touch. His deceiving skills were off the charts. He has the silverware to match, too. That guy has won league titles in Italy and Spain, the Champions League, the World Cup and the European Championship

Billy: That's what you call a decorated player. As a manager he's done well, too. He's won three Champions League trophies. Managerial tekkers right there!

Jez: His playing days are in the past, but there's plenty of hope for tekkers in the future. I think it's going to become bigger and bigger. I mean, there's a new generation coming up in England with unbelievable technique.

Everyone has their favourite type of tekkers. Swaz, knuckleball and whippage are three of our favourite types. What's yours? Single one out and work on it.

Billy: Our ultimate footballer will have a locker full of tekkers. His technique will be unprecedented because he'll have all the tekkers of so many different players. He'll basically be unplayable and anyone who watches him will remember it for the rest of their lives.

Jez: Yes, mate. It's going to be like watching every tekkers master from football history rolled into one player. The opposition might as well not turn up. Come to that, his teammates might as well not turn up. This guy is going to be unstoppable.

Billy: Tekkers!

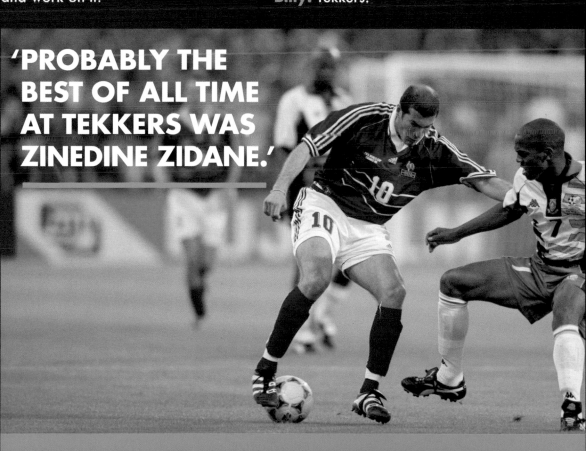

'PROBABLY THE BEST OF ALL TIME AT TEKKERS WAS ZINEDINE ZIDANE.'

TEKKERS

BILLY: **NEYMAR**

9	SPEED
8	VISION
9	TOUCH
8	FINISHING
10	TEKKERS

Jez: Mate, I actually don't know what to say, here. You're lining up to talk tekkers with me and you think any player on the planet will rival Messi?

Billy: Yes, mate.

Jez: I mean, I suppose if you had brought Cristiano Ronaldo to the table then there would be a discussion. And don't get me wrong, Neymar is an incredible talent. But if you're talking tekkers then I think there's no doubt Messi is the man.

Billy: Look, back up a minute, Jez. Everyone knows I'm a huge fan of Ronaldinho. And for my money, Neymar is close to Ronaldinho in so many ways. When you look at his playmaking, his dribbling ability and his all-round tricks, I think this guy holds his own against anyone in the tekkers stakes.

JEZ:
LIONEL MESSI

SPEED	8
VISION	10
TOUCH	10
FINISHING	9
TEKKERS	10

Jez: Calm it, Bill! I'm mostly teasing you, to be honest. I'm the biggest fan of Neymar there is. And I know he's a big fan of Lionel Messi. When he signed for Barcelona he said Messi had inspired him since forever.

Billy: Exactly, so let's just agree that these two guys both have terrific tekkers. That's the beauty of football – it might be a game of opinions but that doesn't mean you have to take sides on everything. Sometimes you can appreciate more than one player at once.

Jez: Very true, mate. But I'm still right. Messi is the king and you know it.

***

THE THANOS

done

Origin: **Invented by Jeremy Lynch, UK**
Skill type: **Dribble**
Difficulty rating: **9**
Tekkers rating: **10**
Frequently used by: **Mr J. Lynch**

Jez: The thing about Thanos is that he's double-hard. And this skill here? Well, it may not be easy. But boy is it worth perfecting. Face up to your opponent. Now it's time to lead him on a merry dance. Tap one way, then drag back past your body as you spin the other way. As the defender shifts his weight to follow you, he'll open his legs. As you spin-out, just touch it between them and you're away. Now that's what I call an Endgame.

1

Tap ball with outside of boot

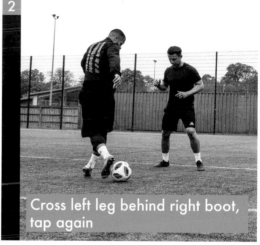

2

Cross left leg behind right boot, tap again

3

Stop ball with right boot

4

Drag the ball back one way, spin the other

'THE THING ABOUT THANOS IS THAT HE'S DOUBLE-HARD.'

5 Trap the ball with the same foot on the other side of your body

6 Drag back, continue spin

7 Tap through defender's legs

8 Accelerate away

9

10

1

2

Cross left leg behind right boot, tap ball

3

Stop ball with right boot

4

Drag ball back one way, spin the other

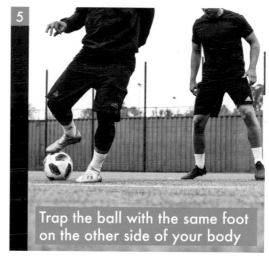

5

Trap the ball with the same foot on the other side of your body

6

Drag back, continue spin

7

Tap through defender's legs. Accelerate

***

THE BERBA

clone

Origin: Invented by Billy Wingrove, UK (nod to Dimitar Berbatov)
Skill type: Dribble
Difficulty rating: 8
Tekkers rating: 8
Frequently used by: Mr B. Wingrove

Billy: Up against a defender who is stronger than you? Don't panic! When you use this piece of skill, it's not your brawn that matters but your brain. Back into the defender as the ball comes to you, flick it up and quickly volley it one way around the defender as you swivel to run the other way. The poor defender won't know who he is or where he's got to, leaving you free to smash it home. Au-Blammo-Yang!

1

Receive the ball with your back to the defender

2

3

Flick the ball up

4

Make sure the ball goes up to the side

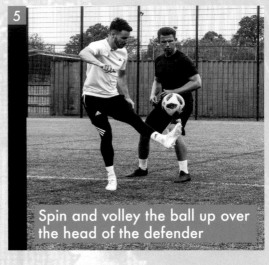

5

Spin and volley the ball up over the head of the defender

6

7

Race around the other side

'THE POOR DEFENDER WON'T KNOW WHO HE IS OR WHERE HE'S GOT TO.'

Good first touch

Bang!

'LEAVING YOU FREE TO SMASH IT HOME.'

* * *

TOUCH TEKKERS DRILL
QUICK TOUCH

This drill improves your control, and your first touch. Become like a baller who can bring a big pass down neatly, like Dele Alli or Olivier Giroud. Once you've got this skill mastered, then your game has moved to a whole new level, because your teammates will be confident to send you a big, big pass, knowing that rather than 'controlling' the ball into row z, you will actually touch it right where you want it. This is another drill you'll benefit from doing with a mate. Ready? Let's go!

Instructions

1. Player A stands inside a circle or a 10 foot x 10 foot square of cones.

2. Player B stands to the side, with the ball.

3. The ball is played in, and Player A has to control the ball deftly. This means a quick touch that kills the ball dead.

4. Vary the height and pace of the delivery to keep Player A on their toes.

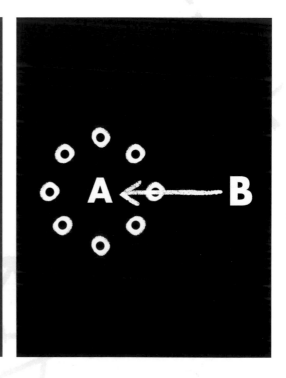

▼ Equipment
Cones.

PRO TIP
Want to go one step better? Make the area smaller, or use a ball launcher to fire it in at an increased height and pace.

VOLLEYS

CHAPTER 5

BILLY VS JEZZA

* * *

VOLLEYS

Jez: I mean, everyone loves a volley. They look amazing! What more is there to say?

Billy: They do look great but there's a lot more to them than just the visuals. They give you a real advantage in attack because, with volleys, you don't need to trap the ball or take an extra touch. This means the opposition's goalkeeper and defenders get less time to prepare and react.

Probably the best volley I've ever seen was Zinedine Zidane's in the Champions League final at Hampden Park in 2002. When the cross came in from Roberto Carlos, the ball was a bit behind Zidane but he had the ability to move his leg back and unleash an absolute beast!

Jez: What a goal. I mean: What. A. Goal. I agree, it's right up there. Another player who is effective with volleys is Zlatan Ibrahimović. That guy is a master volleyer. I'm telling you, for such a tall player, to be able to volley the ball that well is really tough.

Billy: And speaking of tall guys who are good at volleys, we can't overlook Peter Crouch's volley against Man City. It was an absolutely unstoppable shot from 25 yards with unreal dip.

Jez: That was for Stoke, but they were on the other end of a filthy volley when Gareth Bale showed them how it's done. He leaned backwards, arched his foot around the ball and sent it home. I remember when we filmed with Gareth and he talked about that goal.

He also nailed it in the Champions League final against Liverpool. That overhead volley was off the scale and a lot of people said it was even better than Zidane's, who was his coach on the day. So much class.

Billy: So, by now you might be wondering what our tips are for improving your own volley game. To me, a lot of it is about timing and keeping your eye on the ball. Patience is another part of it. In any given match you're likely to get a chance to do your basics: pass, shoot or head. But when it comes to volleys, they are rarer. You might only get the chance to volley once every four or five games. They just don't come around that often.

Jez: So, one technique is to throw the ball, let it bounce once and then shoot. Just keep doing it over and over. The most technical players are usually good at volleys so work on your technique.

There's many flavours of volley: increasingly, players like to hit the ball down into the floor so it bounces up and in. The bounce makes the strike unpredictable and difficult to save. Mesut Özil is big on that one. See which volley takes your fancy most.

Billy: But they're nowhere near as easy as they look. Sometimes people really mess up a volley. We've all done it: you think you're about to smash it into the top of the net but you get it wrong and it ends up more like a rugby conversion.

Jez: Haha! Watch that ball sail RIGHT into outer space!

Billy: But when they come off properly it's brilliant. I loved them when I was growing up. Steven Gerrard always loved a volley, didn't he? Paul Scholes did too – he lashed some absolutely unreal volleys for United. People forget that about him, but go online and you'll see exactly what I mean.

Jez: I'll do that, Bill. In terms of current players look no further than the likes of Kevin De Bruyne and Paul Pogba, who have both pulled off some great little volleys. But here's my question for you: what is a volley? Is this a clear-cut thing?

Billy: Glad you asked, because there's actually quite a heated debate

'RODRÍGUEZ OF COLOMBIA ALSO SMASHED IT INTO THE TOP-LEFT.'

over this. People disagree on whether it can be a volley if the ball has bounced before you hit it, or if you set up the volley yourself by teeing up the ball first. What's your take on this?

Jez: Bill, to be fair I'm too busy enjoying volleys to get too caught up in that. Just sit back and re-watch Benjamin Pavard's goal from the 2018 World Cup finals against Argentina. No wonder it was voted goal of the tournament – it was a cracker!

Billy: I remember it, mate. Straight into the top-left corner! And it was another volley that won the goal of the tournament in 2014 when James Rodríguez of Colombia also smashed it into the top-left. That was an unbelievable strike, too.

Jez: Before we wrap this one up, what other tips have we got on volleys? I think the first thing is to choose well when to try one. Don't try to pull them off all the time. The best opportunity to volley is from a cross or a corner.

Billy: True. Then it's all about your posture. Your non-kicking foot has to be firmly planted so you keep your balance. You'll notice that a lot of players spread their arms out wide when they volley. Again, this helps you keep balance.

Your eyes should be on the ball, because it helps both your poise and balance, which will translate into a cleaner strike. Don't lean back or you're going to sky it. Good luck, guys!

VOLLEYS

BILLY:

LUIS SUÁREZ

8	SPEED
9	VISION
10	TOUCH
10	FINISHING
9	TEKKERS

Billy: Mate, if you're a goalkeeper, one of the most frightening sights in the game must be seeing the ball looping over in the direction of Luis Suárez as he steadies himself ready to volley it top bins.

Jez: Haha, yeah you might as well go home at that point because this guy doesn't miss, does he? I mean, look, I'm enjoying thrashing all this out with you, Bill, but I'm not about to try and argue against Luis actual Suárez's volleys.

We saw it first-hand, didn't we, when we filmed with him. Remind us about that, Bill.

Billy: Certainly, Jez. We challenged him to volley the ball into a washing machine from 20 yards out. I mean, come on, that's a ridiculous challenge. Even the man himself said it would take him several attempts. But then he did it first time!

JEZ:
ZLATAN IBRAHIMOVIĆ

SPEED	8
VISION	9
TOUCH	9
FINISHING	10
TEKKERS	9

He's always ready to shoot quickly and under pressure. Absolutely nothing fazes him. And that's why he's my choice for this category.

Jez: And his movement off the ball is among the best I've ever seen. That's how he scores so many amazing volleys – because first up, he's got himself in the right position to smack it home.

And you know, I think the same is true of Zlatan. His movement and positioning are a big part of his game. And when the ball is headed his way, he has that physicality to really get the most out of the volley. He's almost like an acrobat.

Billy: As England fans know only too well. What about that 30-yard bicycle kick he got for Sweden against us that time? Just… the technique, the accuracy, the confidence. That is tekkers right there. So bold!

PAVARD VOLLEY

done

Origin: **Benjamin Pavard**
Skill type: **Shot**
Difficulty rating: **8**
Tekkers rating: **8**
Frequently used by: **Benjamin Pavard**

Billy: Everyone remembers where they were when they saw Benjamin Pavard perform this naughtiness for France in the World Cup. At first it looked like Lucas Hernandez had overhit his pass, but Pavard struck the ball on the edge of the 18-yard box and fired it home to set France on their way past Argentina. Keep your head over the ball and your weight forward. There's minimum swaz on this one, it's all about the back spin, which makes it fly straight like an arrow. Ooh la la!

1 Ball bouncing towards you

2 Set yourself

3 Lean to the side but keep your weight forward

4 Strike with the outside top of the boot

'THERE'S MINIMUM SWAZ ON THIS ONE, IT'S ALL ABOUT THE BACK SPIN.'

5 Follow through so your striking foot hits the ground first

6 It's a flat shot, hit with back spin

7 It should have hardly any swaz

Bam – top bins!

Always celebrate one of these!

INSIDE THE F2

* * *

F2 TALENT

Jez: So guys, the big news is we've launched our own football talent agency – F2 Talent. We've signed a roster of young players, including the England and Liverpool star Rhian Brewster.

Billy: Yes, Jez! We're really proud of this. We feel like we can really assist young players on all aspects of the game, including the commercial side and how to conduct themselves in certain situations.

I think something we're really, really strong on is how to operate on social media and how to build up a brand.

Jez: And that's a really important part of football today – a lot of players are brands now, and it's a big part of the game.

Billy: That's right, it's not all about the game itself any more. I mean, 90% of it is, of course, but the brand side of things is important. The personal fanbase and Instagram following players can get is huge. Look at someone like Mesut Özil – his online brand is colossal!

Jez: So we feel we're in a good position to tell young players what

LIVERPOOL FOOTBALL CLUB

www.liverpoolfc.com

to do and what not to do on social media. We think we can give them great advice on how to react when you do something wrong.

Billy: We're definitely looking to branch out with projects like this so we can keep busy and relevant long into the future. It's not an exit strategy at all, but we are looking at how we've already made a big difference to kids on YouTube and how we can move into something new, something that's still positive.

A lot of players from the UK and abroad follow us online. If we can help them with advice, I think that's a really positive thing to do. At the moment we're quite busy with other things, but the foundations are there for this side of our work to take off. We've already got loads of younger players that in three to four years' time will be playing at the highest level.

Jez: And Rhian Brewster already is. I honestly think he's going to smash it. Next season will be his season, and I'm not just saying that because he's on our books. The guy is just a natural goal scorer. He scored eight goals at the under-17s World Cup. He was there when the Liverpool team won the Champions League and that would have been an amazing experience for him.

I genuinely think he's going to go on to be one of England's most prolific strikers. I can see it, I can see it. He's a properly cool guy, too. Everyone at Liverpool loves him. Jürgen Klopp loves him. He's got the charisma – his personality is unbelievable. We speak all the time and see each other often.

Billy: He really is amazing. As for the agency, we want to build it but

we want quality more than quantity. The world of football agents is a little murky in parts – there's no point pretending it's not.

Sadly, it's not always the good guy that wins. There are some less-than-good agents out there. That's not to say everyone is like that – there are some exceptions, some wonderful ones. But you get people who become agents with no relevant experience whatsoever.

Jez: Yeah, at times it's been... interesting. Ha ha! There's plenty of snakes and shady stuff going on, but we have to be realistic: that murkiness

isn't going anywhere. We're used to being on the clean-cut side of things. It's actually pretty nice in our usual world, but I don't like the world of football agents so much. Like Bill says, there's nice people too, but everyone knows how things are with agents.

Billy: On a wider level, we're thinking of stripping back some of our wider F2 projects. We need to keep focused on The F2 and the YouTube content that is our bread and butter. We can only stretch ourselves so thin. I think in 2018 we might have stretched ourselves a little too much.

Obviously creating good content is the core of what The F2 is. That's how we keep the brand strong. So over the next two years we are going to make a conscious effort to keep our content strong even if that means stepping away from a few businesses. We want to grow but also keep true to our roots.

Jez: But we're going to carry on with F2 Talent, and it's a pleasure to be working with a new team of guys on that.

Billy: Stay tuned and watch out for our players and watch out for F2 Talent!

DRIBBLING

F2

* * *

CHAPTER 6

DRIBBLING

Billy: Dribbling is something people have stopped doing in recent years because the game has become more about pace and power. So why have we included it in our list of attributes for the ultimate player? Because we predict it's going to make a comeback any day now.

Jez: That's right, we're calling it, right here, right now: dribbling is going to be big again. In my opinion it is one of those skills that makes a player a true great. The likes of Messi, Özil, Ronaldo, Neymar all share that ability to dribble past multiple players and change the game.

Billy: It never completely went away, to be fair...

Jez: True words. And you need dribbling in your locker. You can ping the ball between you and your teammates all day if you're good enough, but sometimes you need to run at opponents with the ball at your feet.
So that's another reason why we've selected dribbling – because it is a crucial part of a team's attacking

options, and because it scares the life out of defenders.

Billy: It does, it really does. If you get this one right, you will terrify your opponents. I see it so often: defenders scared out of their mind because a player is running at them with the ball at his feet. So, Jez, why don't you break down this skill for us? Do you fancy that?

Jez: It would be my pleasure. There are two types of dribbling: running with the ball, which someone like Mbappé is very good at. He'll ping the ball forward and then run onto it. His pace and his brain will mean he nails it.

Then there is dribbling with close control. Here, you need the ability to stop and start, to change direction. This will throw defenders right off the scent. You see it a lot in Europe – guys like Neymar and Messi can do this at the drop of a hat and it's lethal.

Billy: If you want to become lethal, it's really important that you're able to keep the ball stuck to your foot so you can run in different directions. Work on your dribbling and you can learn to go out of your left door or the right door.

If you can dribble at pace the game really opens up for you. Eden Hazard is an example of a player who can really do this. Jadon Sancho is good, too. In fact, when you look at it, the next generation of the England team is blessed with a lot of good dribbling players.

Jez: Every team wants if - someone who can create something out of nothing. Someone who can unlock defences. Someone like Raheem Sterling, who can bring three or four types of dribbling.

When you dribble well you also create space for your teammates. So again, it's really important to have strong dribblers in your team. In this era of tiki-taka football not many top players lose the ball anymore, but every team needs a player who can

run with the ball and create that bit of magic.

Billy: Everyone wants a Neymar.

Jez: Of course they do. You know, Neymar is amazing. I'd actually put his dribbling skills up there with my hero, Ronaldinho, who has praised Neymar.

Billy: Dribbling is something you need a lot of courage for. Look at Mesut

Ozil. His style is to draw players to him to create space behind them. But he gets kicked a lot as a result.

Jez: You have to be brave. Eden Hazard is the most fouled player in the world. But he loves it. Also, with dribbling there is always the danger of fans getting on your back if you get it wrong. So you need to be brave!

Billy: Sterling is a brave guy, isn't he? He's big on how important it is to keep your head up when you're dribbling. That's because you need to see both the opposition players and your own teammates. He also says you need to be able to trick your opponent.

And then, when you've finished your dribble, you need to know what to do with the ball. You need to make the right decision. We'll turn to that in our passing section, so keep a look out!

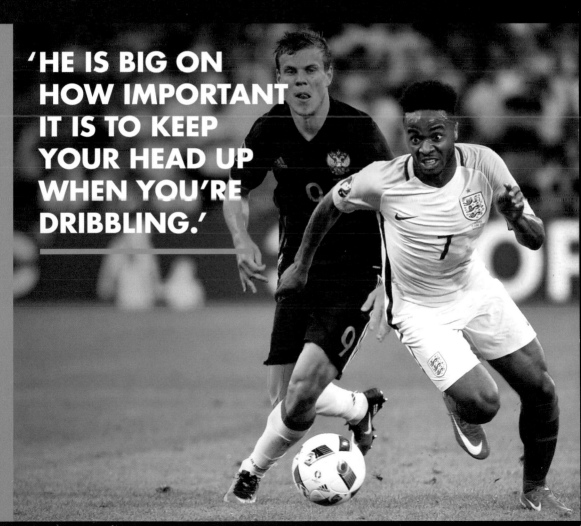

'HE IS BIG ON HOW IMPORTANT IT IS TO KEEP YOUR HEAD UP WHEN YOU'RE DRIBBLING.'

* * *

DRIBBLING

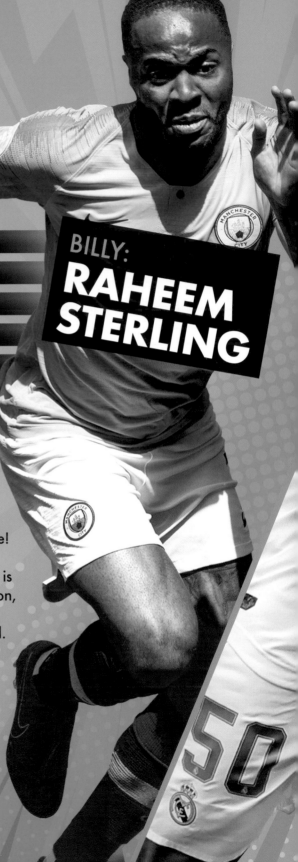

8	SPEED
9	VISION
10	TOUCH
9	FINISHING
10	TEKKERS

BILLY:
RAHEEM STERLING

Jez: If you're going to tell me Eden Hazard isn't the best dribbler of our times then I'm going to have to block you on WhatsApp and every other platform we're connected on.

Billy: Come on, Jez, there's no need for that. At least listen to my thinking first, mate!

Jez: Okay. But I warn you Bill, my thumb is hovering over the 'report and block' button, and I have no fear of pressing that baby. No fear at all. So this had better be good.

Billy: Listen, no one is denying Hazard isn't top, top quality. I'm a fan of the man! But I think when you focus solely on dribbling, Sterling edges it for me.
   He's got that low, low centre of gravity, he's quick and he can dribble like a baby.

Eden Hazard says one of the keys to effective dribbling is to keep defenders guessing what you'll do next. This means you need to be able to beat them on the inside and outside.

JEZ:
EDEN HAZARD

SPEED	9
VISION	9
TOUCH	10
FINISHING	9
TEKKERS	10

Jez: Mate, all of that is true of Hazard.

Billy: Okay, I'm not about to argue. But I think that Sterling edges it because his upper body strength is that much more effective than Hazard's, so in a one-on-one situation he's less likely to get knocked off course. For our ultimate footballer, that's got to be important.

Jez: I'm not arguing with the principles you're using but, come on – Hazard not the best dribbler around? I can't help thinking you're winding me up here! His dribbles are mesmerising and look, Real Madrid don't come knocking for anyone second-rate.

So I don't see why I should even debate this one with you.

Billy: All right, son. No need to get aggro with me.

Jez: You're THIS close to a block, Bill.

NEYMAR
RAINBOW DRIBBLE

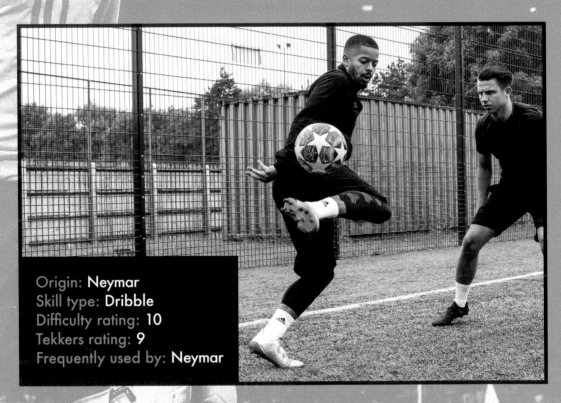

Origin: **Neymar**
Skill type: **Dribble**
Difficulty rating: **10**
Tekkers rating: **9**
Frequently used by: **Neymar**

Jez: Here's your chance to effortlessly beat two defenders in one go. Well, I say effortlessly, but maybe that will be the outcome once you've spent h~~...~~ practising and perfecting ~~...~~ar has pulled this one off lots of times and it's always a treat. It's like he's playing with himself, passing the ball to himself. It's like the Neymar party. Learn this one, F2 family!

Drag the ball back

'LEARN THIS ONE, F2 FAMILY!'

Flick it up with the other foot

As the defender approaches...

Volley the ball over his head using the outside of your boot

'IT'S LIKE THE NEYMAR PARTY.'

Accelerate past the defender

Keep your eye on the ball

You're away!

Drag back

Flick up....

So the ball goes to the side of you

Flip over

GET THE DRILLS

* * *

DRIBBLING DRILL
BALL CONTROL

One of the best sights in football is when you see someone like Raheem Sterling surging upfield or weaving around his opponents with the ball at his feet. It's a tricky skill, but one that can be learned if you put the time in. With our dribbling drill, you will get your speed up, improve your footwork and awareness, and learn to run with your head up. It is particularly useful for when you are dealing in tight spaces.

Instructions

1. Put three cones on the ground in a triangle or line, each one spaced three feet apart.

2. Dribble the ball between the cones.

3. Be sure to use all the surfaces of your boots.

4. Rock some super quick touches to guide the ball around the cones in a controlled pattern.

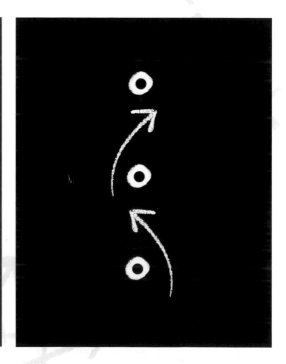

PRO TIP
Ready to get serious? To take it to a new level, simply move the cones so they are even more tightly spaced – how about two feet apart?

FINISHING

CHAPTER 7

BILLY VS JEZZA

*** * ***

FINISHING

Billy: Here Jez, check this out: finishing is important in football because you win matches by scoring more goals than the other side.

Jez: Wow, you're kidding me. Is that how it works? Mind = blown! I'm going to need to take some time to process this. I can't even...

Billy: But seriously, finishing is so important, because even in the best teams you usually won't find yourself in a goalscoring position that many times in one match. So it's vital that when you do, you have the best chance of putting that ball away. That's what will make you our ultimate footballer.

Jez: Yes, it's that sort of player you want leading the line. Take Harry Kane for example – when he gets in a goalscoring position you back him to tuck it away, don't you? He talks a lot about mental strength – he says you have to be 'brave' and keep a 'level head'.

Billy: Same with Mo Salah. And he says that if you want to improve your finishing then you need to spend a lot of time upfront. When he was asked why his finishing rate increased at Liverpool, he said the answer was simple: 'I play closer to the goal than any club before.'

Jez: Haha, you can see what he means, though!

Billy: In the modern game it seems like everyone can use their weaker foot. Way back when, you had right-footed players who couldn't finish with their left foot to save their lives and left-footed players who couldn't finish with their right foot.

Jez: But now if you look at the elite game, most players can at least get by with their weaker foot. One-footed players just aren't accepted anymore. If you want to make it to the top and certainly, if you want to be our ultimate footballer, you're going to need to be able to stick that ball away with either foot.

Billy: Christian Eriksen told us that when he was younger he would consciously use his weaker left foot. He just used it over and over until he was comfortable with it. He made it a strength.

It's important to work on this yourself, because if you have an obviously weaker foot then defenders will 'show you' to the side you're weakest on. By which I mean they will make sure you're having to hit the ball with the foot you're least comfortable with. Then you're immediately at a disadvantage.

Jez: That is good advice, people. So here's some more. You should watch the goalkeeper's position and see if they've left too much of a gap. If so, tuck that ball away pronto.

Keep your eyes on the ball as you hit it and make sure you've gone for the right technique – from the tap-in to the powerful thump, there are lots to choose from. Stay cool and calm, whichever you go for. The most successful finishers are those who can remain composed in the heat of the battle.

Billy: That's right, Jez. The best finishers are those who come alive in that moment. The ones who thrive on the pressure of turning a chance into a goal.

Jez: Over time, the best strikers develop an instinct for finishing. Wayne Rooney is a good example of this and so is Kane. They don't have to think about it – their instinct guides them.

In fact, with some players, the less time they have to think about it the better. I think Raheem Sterling is at his strongest when he relies on his instincts.

Billy: Our ultimate player will always be right among the goals. He'll know that accuracy will always trump power. But he'll also know that power has its own place, too.

Jez: And – as Billy exclusively revealed at the top of this section – you need goals to win matches. So, get out there and practise your finishing. Don't be one of those people who spend their time practising how they will celebrate a goal. No, be one of the people who spend their time practising how to score a goal.

Billy: Got it?

'OVER TIME, THE BEST STRIKERS DEVELOP AN INSTINCT FOR FINISHING. WAYNE ROONEY IS A GOOD EXAMPLE OF THIS AND SO IS KANE. THEY DON'T HAVE TO THINK ABOUT IT – THEIR INSTINCT GUIDES THEM.'

FINISHING

BILLY:
HARRY KANE

8	SPEED
9	VISION
9	TOUCH
10	FINISHING
9	TEKKERS

Jez: Okay, I'm going to start this one by saying club loyalty might have played a part in your choice. Harry Kane is an immense talent but you can't just pick him because he plays for Spurs. This is a serious debate and I'm gonna fight you all the way. Justify your choice, Bill. Justify yourself to the F2 Family!

Billy: Erm, justify saying Harry Kane is a brilliant striker? Give me a tough gig, why don't you? So let's crunch some facts. He's the first player to score 100 goals for the mighty Spurs in the Premier League and the fastest player to score 100 league goals for Spurs. He won the Golden Boot at the 2018 World Cup, he's won it twice at league level. He has an OBE.

Jez: Don't know about the "mighty" Spurs but those are amazing facts. Here's some Sergio stats for you: the youngest player to appear in the Argentinian league,

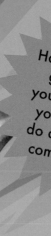

JEZ:
SERGIO AGÜERO

SPEED	8
VISION	9
TOUCH	9
FINISHING	10
TEKKERS	10

the best goals-per-minute ratio in Premier League history, Man City's all-time highest goalscorer. But here's another fact that knocks it out the park: he's won four Premier League titles. I think that last fact is the biggest difference between them. If we're wanting to put together the ultimate footballer, why wouldn't we choose one who has the experience of winning on the biggest stage?

Billy: Ooh, having a dig at the mighty Spurs are we, Gooner? How many Champions League finals have your boys reached recently, Jez? In fact, when was the last time your boys were even in the Champions League?

Jez: ...

JOÃO FÉLIX ONE-ON-ONE

Origin: **João Félix**
Skill type: **Shot**
Difficulty rating: **10**
Tekkers rating: **9**
Frequently used by: **João Félix**

Jez: This one isn't easy but it looks amazing. There's a lot of moves in swift succession so you need your mind and body on top form to nail it. It's one of those skills that make the fans say: what did he do there? They will watch it and re-watch it loads of times before they can see what happened. So give this one a go.

1 Race onto the through ball

2 ... played beyond the last defender

3

4

5 Flip the ball up by rolling your foot over the top of the ball

6 As the keeper goes for it...

7 Flip the ball over the top using the outside of your boot

8 Run past the keeper

9

Bring it down

Smack it into the open net!

HAZARD PANNA

Origin: **Unknown**
Skill type: **Shot**
Difficulty rating: **7**
Tekkers rating: **7**
Frequently used by:
Eden Hazard, Lionel Messi

Billy: This one is pure cheek, guys. As everyone, including the goalkeeper, is wondering whether Hazard is going to put it to the left or the right of the keeper, he sticks it through his legs. He's got no chance at that stage. Our dads used to call it the nutmeg but we're calling it the panna. Why? Because as you may have noticed – we're down with the kids!

1 — Race onto the through ball

2

3 — As the keeper spreads himself

4 — Knock it through his legs

5 — He's got no chance!

'WE'RE DOWN WITH THE KIDS!'

* * *

KANE

clone

SNAPSHOT

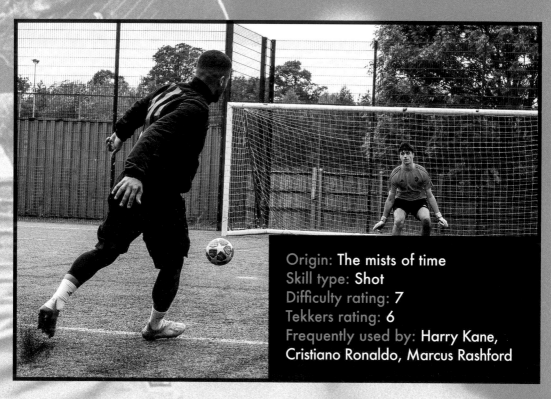

Origin: **The mists of time**
Skill type: **Shot**
Difficulty rating: **7**
Tekkers rating: **6**
Frequently used by: **Harry Kane,
Cristiano Ronaldo, Marcus Rashford**

Jez: How many times have we seen Harry Kane find the back of the net in the blink of an eye? Of all the strikers in the Premier League, he's the one you'd want in that situation. He keeps his head when the pressure is on and you'll need to do the same to pull it off. The trick is to hit it early before the keeper has time to set himself. Don't wait to get too close and find yourself closed down. That way you'll catch him off guard and he'll be picking it out of the net.

1
Before the keeper has time to set himself...

2
Hit it early

3
Leave the keeper stranded

4
It doesn't matter which corner of the net

'CATCH HIM OFF GUARD AND HE'LL BE PICKING IT OUT OF THE NET.'

* * *

WEAK FOOT DRILL
LEFT FOOT, RIGHT FOOT

We love a player who has two feet. You know what we mean? Obviously, all players have two feet, but we mean the ballers who have two strong feet – the guys who are equally comfortable with their left or right peg. This drill will truly increase your ability with your weaker foot and both your passing and shooting skills on your weaker side. Sounds good, right?

Instructions

1. Set the rebound net on the edge of the box

2. Play the ball against it with your weak foot.

3. Receive the ball back and finish into the goal with your weak foot.

4. Vary using your left foot or right foot.

5. Repeat 10 sets of four reps.

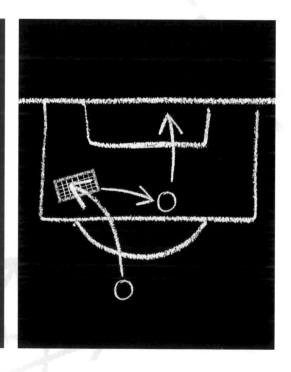

▼ Equipment
Rebound net. (You can use a wall if you haven't got one, or simply lay the ball off to a mate!)

ACADE

PRO TIP
Run a challenge between you and your friends – who can score most with a weak foot?

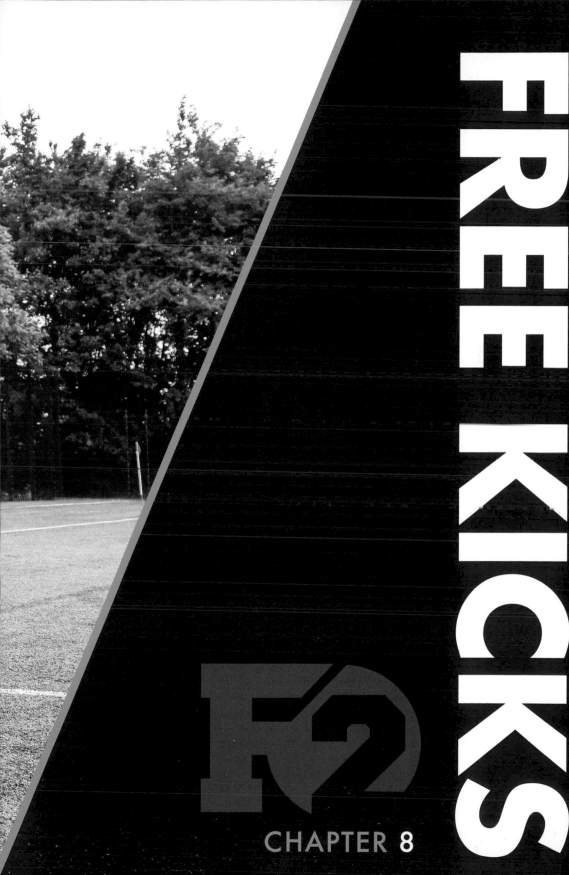

FREE KICKS

CHAPTER 8

***

FREE KICKS

Billy: Let's get straight what we're talking about here. Free kicks can be awarded anywhere on the pitch, but the ones we're going to focus on are the free kicks in the danger zone. And there's no two ways about it: having someone great at them gives you that extra chance to score. The ultimate player will be devastating from set pieces.

Jez: And you really, really need to put in the hours on this one. Sometimes there will only be two or three free kick opportunities in a whole 90-minute match. So you can't afford to have a low success rate with them. You need that ratio to be high.

So, get working, people! The good news is that this is one of the areas of the game where you don't really need anyone else to help – you can work on it completely by yourself. So whether you're good is going to be determined mainly by your work ethic.

There's no hiding here, people. It's that 10,000 hours thing I've talked about before. Have you practised free kicks for hours? If not, you can't expect to be a master at it.

Look at David Beckham. He stayed back after training to practise free kicks, and you saw the fruits of that in so many important matches for club and country. The same goes for Cristiano Ronaldo – he's always first to training and last to leave. A lot of that time he's practising free kicks. And that's why he's scored so many on the biggest stage.

Billy: Exactly. You want to get yourself to a level where, statistically, you've got more chance of hitting the target than not. If you're hitting the target only one time out of 10 in practice, that's cool. Keep practising. But if you're only hitting the target one time out of 10 in practice then don't try a free kick in a match. Lots of teams have that one player who insists on taking all the free kicks even though he's not that good at them. Don't be that guy.

Jez: Seriously. Don't be that guy.

Billy: Just don't.

Jez: You want to be hitting the target six or seven times out of 10 in practice before you even think of taking free kicks in a match. Because then you know that statistically the odds are in your favour to get it right.

There are different types you can attempt. The whippage technique is possibly the safest. I see it as like an extended form of a penalty. You

can deceive the keeper, just like you do with a pen. Cristiano Ronaldo, Neymar, and Zlatan Ibrahimović love a bit of that action.

Billy: Ronaldinho was so good at that too.

Jez: Bill, do you have to bring that guy into everything?

Billy: Yes, I think I do to be honest.

Jez: Haha, fair enough I suppose, he is a legendary baller!

Billy: So, if you want to trick the keeper in a match, get a teammate to stand over the ball with you. This makes the keeper unsure which side to pick and when you're going to kick the ball. Or you can stick players in the wall to block the keeper's field of view. If he can't see the moment the ball is struck, he won't be able to react so well.

Jez: Have you noticed how Ronaldo stands that same way before every free kick? Have you ever wondered why? I mean, obviously, he's focusing and shuffling out anything that will distract him.

But it's also about muscle memory. If he stands like that every time he's about to take a free kick, whether that's in training or in a match, his body and mind get attuned to knowing that it's showtime. That it's time to nail it.

So you can try to incorporate a bit of that into your game. Don't worry what people think. Just follow the best and become the best you can be.

And as well as Ronaldo, you should observe Lionel Messi. That guy alone has scored more goals directly from free kicks in Europe's top leagues than every side (except Juventus) since the beginning of 2011–12. Every side! It's just unreal.

Billy: That's the level we want for our ultimate footballer. That's what we're looking for.

He's coming together well, isn't he?

***

FREE KICKS

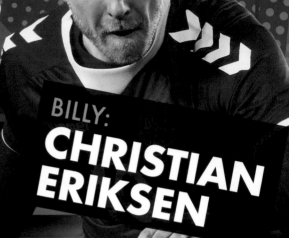

7	SPEED
9	VISION
8	TOUCH
9	FINISHING
8	TEKKERS

BILLY: CHRISTIAN ERIKSEN

Billy: Jezza, name me a player in the Premier League who you would rather have lining up to take a free kick other than Christian Eriksen.

Jez: But I want to talk about Paulo Dybala. So let me ask the question this time: do you rate Lionel Messi and do you rate Andrea Pirlo?

Billy: Of course I do. What are you driving at, Jez?

Jez: Well, the pundits in Italy are absolutely nuts about Dybala. They have compared him to both Messi and Pirlo, and I think you have to admit that when you've got those two guys rolled into one, you're onto a proper winner.

We can pick out so many spectacular free kicks this guy has scored at the highest level, but probably the best one he will ever score was in a charity match. Practically every player in the opposition lined up in the wall right in front of the goal line. Because it was a charity match, even fans started running onto the pitch to join the wall.

PRO TIP
Christian Eriksen says a lot of what you need is in your head rather than your legs. He says if you are smart enough you don't need to run.

JEZ:
PAULO DYBALA

SPEED	7
VISION	8
TOUCH	8
FINISHING	9
TEKKERS	8

Billy: Yes, Jez! I've seen that one. Some of the wall even hung from the crossbar, to make it even tougher. They were determined to shut him out!

Jez: Exactly, but he managed to put the ball in the only spot left unguarded, despite everything – and that, my friends, is a free kick wizard.

Billy: It is. I've got to say, he is class. My favourite Eriksen free kick came quite early in his Spurs career. At Sheffield United he scored an absolute beauty. He curled in a stunning 25-yarder off the inside of the post.

Jez: So how are we going to decide this? How can we separate two absolute legends, Bill?

Billy: You know what, Jez? I think the only way would be to have a free kick-off. Each of them gets 10 chances from various angles and we see who comes out on top. Maybe it could be an F2 video.

Jez: Would watch, mate. Would totally watch that!

KROOS
clone
FREE KICK

Origin: Tony Kroos
Skill type: Shot
Difficulty rating: 8
Tekkers rating: 7
Frequently used by: Tony Kroos

Billy: Here's a free-kick technique that is mind-blowing when it comes off. Tony Kroos nailed it on the highest stage when he did it at the 2018 World Cup. It was lined up from a narrow angle, so everyone expected him to knock it near post for a teammate to touch it in. But instead he tapped the ball to Marco Reus, who cushioned it for Kroos to curl it perfectly into the far corner of the net. You weren't expecting that, were you? Neither were the opposition!

1

Free-kick out wide

2

Roll the ball to your teammate

3

To get you a better angle

Run up at 90 degrees to the ball

Strike with your instep

7

Follow through for maximum swaz!

8

* * *

MESSI SOFT SCOOP

Origin: **Lionel Messi**
Skill type: **Shot**
Difficulty rating: **9**
Tekkers rating: **9**
Frequently used by: **Lionel Messi**

Billy: We all like a bit of soft scoop when we're on a day out at the beach. Ideally in a nice cone with a stick of chocolate in it. But Lionel Messi prefers his soft scoop on the football pitch. This is almost a Panenka free kick. Like the Panenka, it's all about disguise. It's a skill well worth learning because you can completely bamboozle the goalkeeper. He'll have no idea where the ball is going and that 'where' might end up being the back of his net.

1 Approach at 45 degrees

2 Fake the big hit

3 Instead stab your foot underneath the ball

4 Almost like a panenka

5

6 The keeper is completely wrong-footed

7 And left stranded

8

9 As the ball floats in

1 Fake

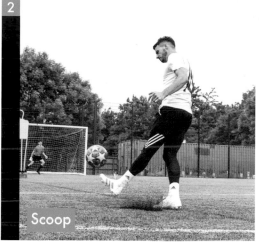

2 Scoop

3 Float

HEADING

CHAPTER 9

* * *

HEADING

Billy: You can use them to stop goals or score goals – where would we be without headers?

Jez: Very true, the perfect header is a true art form if you can get it right.

Billy: What can I say, Jez? I'm a fan! So, let's look into why headers are important and what it takes to be the best at them.

The first truth-bomb I'm going to drop here is that you don't need to be tall to be good at heading the ball. I mean, look, it's true that Peter Crouch got in the Guinness World Records book for the most headed goals scored in the Premier League. But Crouchie would say himself: you don't need to be a giant to be knocking the headers in.

Jez: That's right. For a start, if you're small you're going to have more of a chance with diving headers. If you want to pull off a diving header and you're Crouchie's size, it's going to take you about three years to get down low enough to meet the ball with your nut!

Billy: Exactly. It's simply not the case that heading is all about being tall, because it's actually all about timing and awareness. Heading from a corner is about movement. Smaller players can still jump high if they time it right. Don't worry about your height, just focus on your timing and technique. Read the flow of the ball. Watch players who are good at headers and see what they do.

Jez: Yes mate, look at Sergio Agüero who is only five foot eight – his movement is outstanding. He can read the cross. But obviously, some height isn't going to hurt, is it? You've got Diego Costa, who is six foot one. Olivier Giroud is six foot three. He is an outstanding header of the ball but even though he's tall, so much of his ability in the air comes from his movement rather than his height.

Billy: Yeah, there are tall players who are bad at heading and small players who are good at heading. Basically, heading is important all over the pitch. From defenders clearing their lines to strikers getting up and heading the ball. Watch games and spot the guys who are good with their heads. See what they do. Check out the likes of Virgil van Dijk, Sergio Ramos and Nathan Aké.

Jez: And there are so many types of header. As a striker, you may be looking at the cushioned header. You're there with your back to goal and you cushion a header down to your attacking midfielder.

Then there's the diving header, where you throw yourself across the defender. And what about the looping header at the back post? Or the rocket header, where a lot of it is about your neck muscles? So many different flavours of header. See which you are best at.

Cristiano Ronaldo loves a header, doesn't he? I remember when he scored against Wales. He jumped so high I thought he was going to take off and end up in space! The man's got so much spring! He was two foot six inches off the ground which, added to his height, means he was at eight foot seven inches. Having got that high, he delivered a bullet header at 71.3kph.

Billy: Now that is proper heading – try and deal with that!

Jez: At the other end of the field you've got another maestro of the defensive header we just talked about: Van Dijk. Well, he's good with

the head at both ends, to be fair. He's smashed some in for Liverpool. In recent years there were the likes of John Terry, Rio Ferdinand and Nemanja Vidić – they stand out as examples of players who were really effective at headers.

Billy: The most spectacular header is the diving header. I feel like diving headers are all about instinct. They're sort of the same as a bicycle kick. It's just an instinctive, impulse-driven thing. It's like your body has made the decision rather than your mind. So, with that one, don't think about it. Just do it!

Jez: Let's make sure our ultimate footballer is good with his head. We'll be wanting him winning balls in the air all over the pitch and certainly knocking in a few goals with his head too.

You know what, Bill? Heading the ball is actually pretty cool when you get it right.

***

HEADING

BILLY:
ROBERT LEWANDOWSKI

8	SPEED
7	VISION
8	TOUCH
9	FINISHING
7	TEKKERS

Billy: Lewandowski is just one of those players who, when you picture them in your mind, is always heading the ball, right? He's an amazing talent and he's got the works in his locker. Including being a big-game player. He can nut them in on the biggest stage!

He's got the right height and technique to be amazing in the air. Like we said earlier, height isn't essential for effective heading but it certainly doesn't hurt.

Jez: Yeah, but it's the same with Van Dijk. These guys are exceptional talents and heading really is the strongest thing in their armoury. The Dutchman's ability in the air is top drawer as far as I'm concerned. Just look at how amazing he is at set pieces.

He won the most aerial duels in the Champions League last season and that says it all. When you're rocking facts like that on the highest stage, you

Virgil van Dijk says it's important to develop confidence. He says he has worked hard to eliminate nerves from his game because he felt they limited him. So be bold!

SPEED	8
VISION	9
TOUCH	8
FINISHING	7
TEKKERS	8

BILLY:
VIRGIL VAN DIJK

know you're the man. I actually think he's got the works.

Billy: Look, that's a great fact. You make a powerful argument, Jez. But at the end of the day, my man Lewandowski has got something on his CV that your guy hasn't. He scored five goals in nine minutes. Van Dijk is an absolute hero and I love him to bits. But until he has something like that to put on the table, I think my man edges it. End of.

Jez: Eh? You're going to go all 'end of' on us? Erm, okay…

* * *

HEADER DRILL

HEAD FIRST

We all love it when we see a player who is the master of the header. Whether it's Cristiano Ronaldo leaping halfway to the moon in attack, or Virgil van Dijk clearing the lines at the back with his head, it's a brilliant skill to work on. This drill teaches you to win your aerial battles and to time your jump to perfection. Let's get going!

Instructions

1. Lay out some mannequins in the goal mouth.

2. Get a mate to serve the ball above the mannequin.

3. The heading player has to get over the mannequin to head the ball to safety, or into the goal.

4. Repeat six sets of four reps each time you practise.

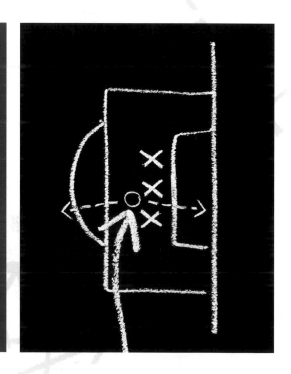

▼ Equipment
Don't have a mannequin? Then you can use a mate instead to stand in, or simply jump and head the ball at its highest point, unopposed.

PRO TIP
Concentrate on technique and accuracy first. Power can be added later.

* * *

F2FC

Billy: A big dream of ours came true when we formed our own football team: F2FC. We've built an incredible squad mixing promising academy players with celebrities and social influencers.

We've got quite a few celebrity friends through what we do and we're mates with a lot of young players so the team itself formed fairly quickly.

Jez: Yeah, it's something we've been thinking about for a while. I think it's really nice for our fans because it gives them the chance to come and watch us play.

But it still takes organisation, and Sam Bayford has really helped us set it up. He's the team manager and he's done so much to help us to recruit players.

We've beaten all the well-known YouTube teams and done the whole competitive approach. So we decided we wanted to approach it in a more positive way, that goes beyond just beating other teams.

Now, each time we play, it will be for a charity. The focus will be not so much on winning but the good that comes from us playing football.

Billy: The match at Old Trafford against Tango Squad FC was unreal for so many reasons.

Jez: Yeah, not least your goal, Billy. It's unbelievable that the first goal for the F2 is basically the same as Lionel Messi's first goal for Barcelona. We pushed on from there, really.

We got the win in the end but it was a hard game. We'd hardly played together so it was tough, really tough as a game. But how great is it to have played at Old Trafford?

Billy: An amazing experience. I didn't do the Messi goal on purpose, I must admit, but I'll take it nevertheless. It was just an unbelievable moment to score at Old Trafford. To get the goal and get the win was just incredible and what a way to launch the F2FC as well.

I liked wearing the armband and leading the team out, too. Luckily I didn't have to wrestle with Jez for the captaincy. He is just so relaxed and chilled, he's not fussed either way. He was just like: 'Have it'. He wanted to give me that moment, which was very nice of him. So I just took it straight away!

Jez: Yes, definitely straight away. Never seen you take something so quick, ha ha. But seriously, there was no big discussion about which of us would lead the team out. We're not too fussed about it. It was more, 'Do you want to take it? You take this one and I'll take it next time.' It's that sort of thing – taking turns.

He was wearing the armband and doing the tactics with Sam at half-time, so maybe Billy's got an eye on management in the future. I know he enjoys that side of things more than me. What do you say, Bill?

Billy: Bill says yes! I love coaching and I'd love to be a manager, I really would. I don't know when exactly but eventually I would love to be one. I love getting the best out of people. I like the prospect of it: treating every single person like an individual entity within a team game.

There's loads of strategies for that, so I would really love the challenge of being a coach or manager someday. I just don't know when – but definitely in the future.

Jez: I'd like that, mate. In the meantime, we're over the moon to have the F2FC. They're top lads. The camaraderie and team spirit are unbelievable. It's not just us two as players – it's not all about us. It's actually really nice for us to have the team vibe because we're normally working as a duo – we miss the banter you get when you're part of a bigger team.

We've got that now with F2FC. Everyone is at the same level. No one talks down or up to anyone. We all respect each other just the same. We are all just players in the same team. It's actually really lovely.

And I think pretty soon we might get some legends playing for us. There's a lot of stars who like keeping on playing and staying fit. The F2FC is the perfect outlet for that. Watch out for us!

TACKLING

CHAPTER 10

BILLY VS JEZZA

***

TACKLING

Jez: You know what? I think reading the game must be the most underappreciated attribute in football.

Billy: I agree with that, it's so true mate. Being able to read the game well really puts you one step ahead of everyone. You always know what's going to happen next, before the defenders.

This means you don't necessarily have to have so much pace, because your intelligence gets you there. Players like Bernardo Silva at Man City and Luka Modrić at Real Madrid aren't fast, but they always get in the right positions to do damage.

For this, it's absolutely vital to be on the same wavelength as your teammates. It's hard to have vision unless you're on the same wavelength. You need to know what they want.

So if Jez has the ball, he needs to know what sort of pass I want. If we're on the same wavelength, all I've got to do is show my body shape or a bit of eye contact and he'll know what to do.

Jez: Some players have it naturally, but I think experience, studying the game and good coaching will take you a long way. Look at guys like Zidane, Pirlo, Xavi and Iniesta for examples to follow. It's important. You see it all the time – it's small margins in football between greatness and failing. It can come down to milliseconds and those can come down to how fast you read the game.

This is where tackling comes in. For example, if you read the game well it can make the difference between winning the ball cleanly or wiping out the opponent and giving away a free kick or penalty. And that could cost your team the match.

Billy: Or equally, instead of getting your toe onto a great ball across the six-yard box, you end up sliding into the net while the ball goes out for a throw-in. It's the same thing.

Jez: Listen, the technique between those at the top of the game and the semi-pros, a lot of the time it's very similar. There are players who are playing in non-league who are very similar to some Premier League players. But you will very rarely find non-league players who will read the game better than Premier League players. It is one of the major differences between the best and the rest.

Positional sense is also really important, so part of reading the game is making sure you avoid encroaching on a teammate's space. You need that understanding. It's no good if you are getting in each tackle at the same time!

Billy: With tackling, it's important to get up quickly. You need that agility. And if you can read which way the player's going to go, that's half the battle won. Timing is key, as Jez said. If you are even a millisecond late, the ball's gone and you could be headed for an early bath.

Jez: There are many types of tackle. John Terry was an absolute master at the slide tackle. Or there's the tackle where you just kind of nick the ball. Van Dijk is one of the best right now, and Sergio Ramos remains at the top of the game in this category.

Billy: For our ultimate player we want a guy who can nail all these

ackles. We want him winning the ball all over the field so the opponents don't have a chance. And the key to him getting those tackles right will be his ability to read the game.

Jez: Yes mate, we want him to read the game the way the kid in the corner of the library reads books. And if you want to work on this attribute yourself,

you should spend time studying matches at all levels of football. If you're watching on TV, watch the game a few times. If you're at the ground, sit or stand as high up as you can so you can see everything.

Just take note of the positional play of everyone on the field. You'll be reading the game as they read the game!

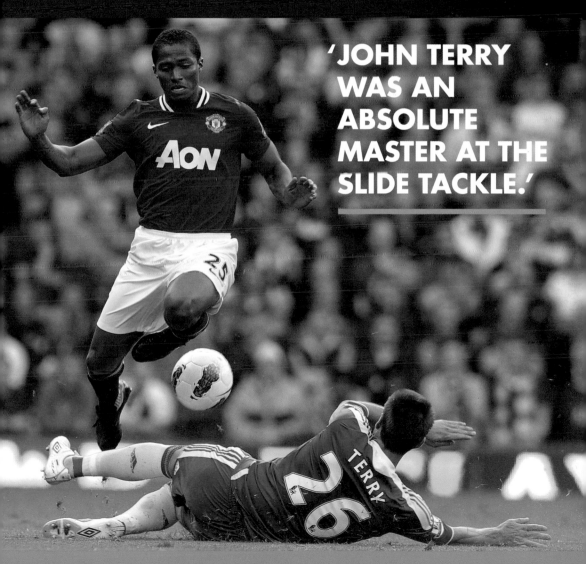

'JOHN TERRY WAS AN ABSOLUTE MASTER AT THE SLIDE TACKLE.'

TACKLING

9	SPEED
9	VISION
8	TOUCH
8	FINISHING
10	TEKKERS

Jez: There's so many different qualities you need to be a great tackler. Chiellini has got them all. He's brave, aggressive and strong. He has good awareness and razor-sharp positional sense. Also, he can read the game so well that he is already a step ahead of his opponents before it comes to the tackle.

Billy:: Same with Ramos. For me, Ramos shades it on technical prowess. I think he's practically exploding with tekkers, I really do. He's also versatile – he can smash it in centre-midfield as well as central defence.

Jez: Yeah, and 'smash it' is a good way of putting it. He doesn't muck about, does he, and he's picked up some cards down the years, haha!

Billy: That's right, Jez. But that's the thing about tackling – it's not for the faint-hearted, is it? For me, I want the tackling in my team to be uncompromising. And certainly for our Ultimate Footballer, he'll need to pull no punches.

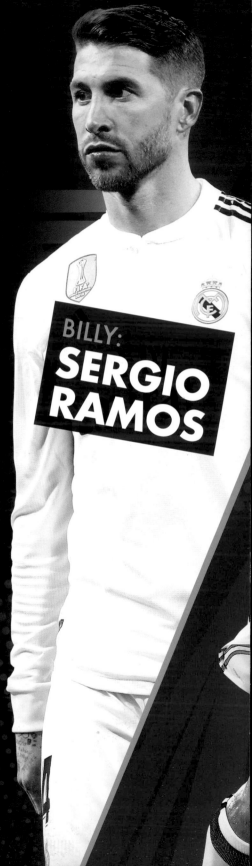

BILLY:
SERGIO RAMOS

JEZ:
GIORGIO CHIELLINI

SPEED	8
VISION	9
TOUCH	8
FINISHING	6
TEKKERS	9

And if you want the proof Ramos is the ultimate tackler then I offer you the words of one Neymar da Silva Santos Júnior. He was asked who's the best defender he ever came across and he named Ramos. Jezza, we have a winner.

Jez: Not so fast. Chiellini is a commanding tackler, and I reckon if Neymar had faced him more times there's a chance he might have chosen him. José Mourinho has really singled him out, and you know when José praises someone, he means it – he's not one to dole out kind words for nothing, is he?

Billy: Fair words. One thing I think we can both agree on: if we were running with the ball we wouldn't want to see either of them coming into view, would we?

GET THE DRILLS

* * *

TACKLING DRILL
BLOCK MASTER

Do you want to tackle like a Ramos, a Van Dijk or a Matić? This drill will take you a long way there. It really improves your tackling and responses. So, get working on this one and you will be agile and able enough to be a rock for your team. You'll be whipping the ball off your opponents like a pro. Guys, we're actually scared of the monster you might become!

Instructions

1. Set up for a blocking session, with three mannequins 10 yards apart.

2. Player A tries to hit one of three mannequins.

3. Player B has to try and deflect away.

4. Player A is all about making the hit, whilst Player B, the defending player, tries to stop them.

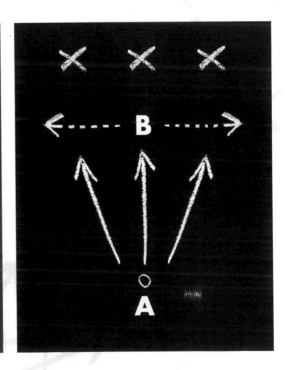

PRO TIP
Get back up as quickly as possible after each block attempt, regardless of whether you've stopped the ball or not. It's crucial to be ready for the next attempt.

* * *

COLLABORATING

PART ONE

N'Golo Kanté

Jez: Here's a simple fact for you: it's impossible to meet N'Golo Kanté and not like him. If you do dislike him then there's something wrong with you. Seriously, he's possibly the nicest guy in football.

Billy: The guy was the nicest and most approachable, gentle footballer you could ever meet. He's just so polite and nice. Not loud at all, despite his unbelievable talent.

Jez: That's a good point.

Billy: Kanté is very chilled. He just smiles all the time. It was a freezing cold day when we met him, but I'll always remember that when he turned up, he was so positive. I've never met a footballer with the aura he had. He's totally humble.

I can't explain it. He has no right to be shy but he is exactly that. There's something almost yogic or Zen about him. It's true serenity.

Jez: These collaborator shoots go well because the players know us and respect what we're trying to do. So they know we won't come after them, or do anything bad.

Billy: That's exactly it, Jez. They know we're simply trying to get the

best out of them. I think when we do these shoots, it's important we try and play to their strengths. So if they're shy like Kanté, we won't want to press them to talk too much. If they're funny, we want to try and get that out of them. We want to show the best side of them.

So when we meet Kanté we just play to his strengths. He's got an engine on him and he's a great footballer. It's all about knowing the player and identifying what content would suit each player.

Jez: We did the Cold Blooded Challenge with him. The Cold Blooded Challenge is brilliant. It's where one of us is popping off shots from the edge of the box, while the other one is trying to distract him, using any means that they can think of.

This time, it was me and Kanté vs Billy and César Azpilicueta. It was fierce! Billy brought a bit of fire to the dance, but that wasn't a problem. It was never going to faze us. We blew leaves at them. They had artificial snow falling on us. There was even an eagle flying across the face of the goal – the works. But me and Kanté came out on top. It was fun, man.

Isco

Jez: We loved filming with Isco. He was a great example of a player who was really up for filming and having fun. He wasn't in a rush to go away. Obviously everyone knows his touch is one of the best in the world, but he's also a really nice guy.

Billy: Jez, tell me this: when we started filming with players all those years ago, could you have dreamt we'd end up filming with so many stars, year-in, year-out?

Jez: I have to be honest and say yeah, I did. Because I've always thought that we are the best in the world when it comes to getting content from players.

Some people will misinterpret that as arrogance, but it's not. I just know we are good at what we do. Everyone is great at something and we've found

what we're great at. We've also worked hard at it. So, yeah, it makes sense to me that we've had so many players make content with us.

Billy: I have to be honest, I wouldn't have dreamed of it getting as big as it has. From my point of view, it's just kind of… happened.

But what's crazy about it is that we're now in a place where I believe there's no footballer in the world we wouldn't be able to film with.

I believe that if you take literally anyone who is a great footballer, we are in a position to collaborate with them, whether it's through a sponsorship, a connection, or just because they're fans of our channel. It's genuinely crazy it's got to that level!

For a while, we were establishing ourselves and having to feel our way a bit on how to get access to the stars. But now, almost every player is a possibility. Whether it's through a brand, or a video, or because they want to boost their social media, they want to work with us.

Isco was a joy to work with. Like Kanté, he's a quiet and calm guy. Or maybe it's just that Spanish mentality, as guys from there always seem to be calm and in control. They go about life at a steady pace. Anyway, his touch was immense on the day. He's just a top guy – I hope he comes to Spurs.

ENGINE

CHAPTER 11

BILLY VS JEZZA

ENGINE

Billy: So, what is an engine? Do you want to get the ball rolling on this one, Jez?

Jez: Yes mate. Put simply, a player with a good engine is one who always gives 100% for the full 90 minutes. It's someone full of energy who works for every second of the game. Someone like Dani Alves or N'Golo Kanté. You know, if you cut those guys open I wouldn't be surprised if you found a V12 in their chests!

Billy: Don't go cutting anyone open, Jez. People don't like that sort of thing.

Jez: Wasn't planning on it, Bill.

Billy: Good to know. An engine is important because it means you can get around the pitch throughout a match. It's especially important in today's game. Managers who like a pressing game want players who can work hard and recover the ball. Your Peps and Klopps are after that sort of guy – one who can last the course.

Jez: That's right. An engine is all about your fitness and your stamina. How long can you go before you burn out and lose all your energy?

And you know what? There's not really any outfield position where that kind of stamina isn't useful. A lot of people know that central midfielders need it but now it's gone beyond that. For instance, full-backs are more like wingers nowadays so they've got to get up and down the pitch.

If you're looking for players with an incredible work rate, Kanté really is the best in recent years. That guy covers so much ground it's unreal. He can pop up at the front and then at the back.

Billy: These sorts of players are sometimes underrated. We talk so much about skill but without an engine player your team is nothing. Imagine buying yourself a brand-new car. It's got all the amazing gadgets and whatnot: cruise control, the works. The only trouble is it hasn't got much beneath the bonnet, so it can't go anywhere.

Jez: Not much use, eh?

Billy: You know, when I played, the opposition sometimes put a man-marker on me. I played a couple of games where I got marked tightly. I didn't worry about it because in my mind I thought: I'll run for 60 minutes until this guy is burned out.

So I just kept running and running. Then, 60 minutes in, I could see my defender was struggling so that was when I made my move. And it worked!

Jez: There are definitely things anyone can do to improve their engine. You can pick up tips by listening to the pros. Jordi Alba, the Barcelona and Spain full-back, is a guy with superb stamina. He says it's important to 'feed your engine'. He says he feeds his by making sure he gets the right food before and after a game. Before a game he advises pasta with chicken, turkey or fish. After the game he says carbohydrates and protein are just as important.

Billy: Jordan Henderson also talks about the importance of diet for the game. He says you really need to 'fuel up' for it. When you eat the right food it's like you're putting petrol in a car.

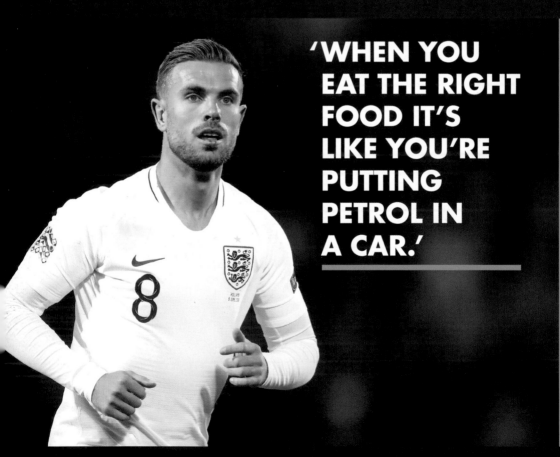

'WHEN YOU EAT THE RIGHT FOOD IT'S LIKE YOU'RE PUTTING PETROL IN A CAR.'

Strengthening your body in a gym will help too, he reckons. That's good advice – do drills to build your stamina so you are on your game for the whole 90 minutes. Open up that window late in the game when you can make your mark.

Jez: And you know, when you look at kids growing up, the engine becomes more and more important every year of their development. Fitness and durability are critical for 11-a-side.

It's the fittest players who come good in the last 20 minutes of matches, just like Bill was talking about.

Billy: One more thought from me on this one: size doesn't matter. To be a hard runner you don't need to be big. Take someone like Rakatić: he's small but his engine and power are top-notch. Players like him are box-to-box, working their socks off and they're absolutely vital. If you want to build the ultimate footballer, you'll want him to have a good engine.

Jez: I can guarantee you this: the way the game is going you will never, ever regret putting time into developing your engine. And that's why this attribute has to be in the make-up of our ultimate footballer.

ENGINE

BILLY:
N'GOLO KANTÉ

7	SPEED
8	VISION
8	TOUCH
7	FINISHING
9	TEKKERS

Billy: Look, to me there's no contest on this one. The greatest engine in football is Kanté. Everyone knows that. The moment you start discussing engines, he's the first name that comes up.

It's the same the other way round, isn't it? If you're talking about Kanté, you immediately mention his engine. Jez mate, whichever way you go about it, Kanté is the man for this attribute.

But I'll still give you 10 out of 10 for your choice of Ndombele. Can't be easy for a Gooner to pick a player from the mighty Spurs!

Jez: Okay, so I've got a lot to come back on here. Firstly, of course I don't mind praising a Spurs player. Just because I support Arsenal it doesn't

JEZ:
TANGUY NDOMBELE

SPEED	8
VISION	7
TOUCH	8
FINISHING	7
TEKKERS	8

make me blind to players from any other team. I don't roll that way.

Secondly, Ndombele is being called 'the next Kanté' for a reason. Your man is rocking it now, but mine is the up-and-coming engine legend. He's also got everything you need to boss it from box to box.

I honestly think that if we look back on this in one year's time, we'll see Ndombele has equalled or even usurped the mighty Kanté.

Billy: Big words, Jez. But I'm not going to fight you on this one. As a Spurs fan I'm just going to hope you're right. Having the next Kanté at the new ground – life at the Lane just got even more interesting!

GET THE DRILLS

* * *

STAMINA DRILL
BOX RUN

When you think about stamina you think about players like N'Golo Kanté – guys who can keep playing at top, top intensity throughout the 90 minutes. So, if you want to be like him, then you've come to the right page! This drill is all about how quickly you can recover, because in a big match, you will need to be able to move quickly even if you're tired. So, getting practise in to recover fast from your runs is crucial to upping your skills.

Instructions

1. Start at one 18-yard box.

2. Run (not sprint) to the other 18-yard box.

3. Then rest for 15 seconds.

4. Then run again!

5. We suggest doing this five times in a session.

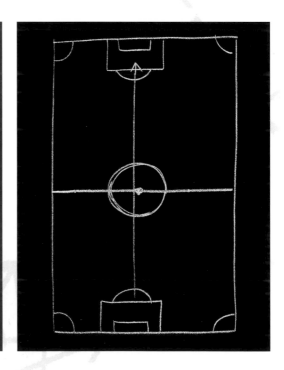

▼ **Equipment**
None needed – just a field or pitch.

PRO TIP
To turbo-charge this drill, you can reduce your recovery time. Start with 15 seconds, then 12, then 10. Or, you can increase the length of the run. So, say you started by running to the halfway line, then next you can run to the box, then all the way to the touchline.

PRO TIP
Four minutes of workout has been proven to be the best way to train!

GET THE DRILLS

* * *

STAMINA DRILL
STAYING POWER

With this stamina drill, we're re-introducing the ball because, no matter how high your endurance levels are, if you're not also handy with the ball then it's not going to be much use on the field. You want to win football matches, not marathons! So here's one that will up your staying power and your baller skills.

Instructions

1. Jog slowly along the long sides of the penalty box.

2. Sprint along the short sides of the box.

3. Get a mate to kick the ball from the penalty spot.

4. You come in to receive the ball.

5. Pass it back to your mate.

6. Sprint away.

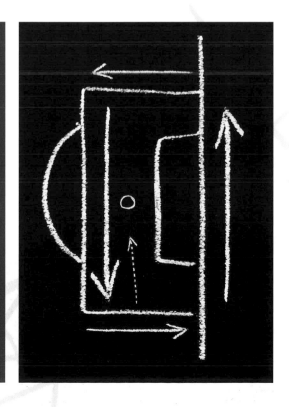

* * *

COLLABORATING

PART TWO

Gareth Bale

Jez: For the second time we got to shoot a video with the legendary Gareth Bale and we had a proper laugh doing it. It was probably the most we've ever laughed on any video. It was just joke after joke after joke. He'd give us a bit of a ribbing, we'd all have a laugh about it.

Billy: Exactly – I'm a Spurs fan and a pacey winger so he was my idol when he was at Spurs. I always pretended to be Gareth Bale, even as an adult.

He's a really nice guy, and we even got a message from his agent saying he loved it and wanted to film again in the future.

His banter was excellent. He was up for a laugh. The only way I can put it is that it was like a group of mates having banter on a football pitch. We felt so comfortable with each other. It didn't feel like being with a £100m footballer. It felt like three mates hanging out together. It was amazing.

Jez: We're actually in a real sweet spot at the moment because the legends have got kids and most of their children are old enough

to watch our videos. We played a legends game recently and Del Piero came up to us and said, 'my son loves your stuff.'

Billy: Yes, that was unreal. This is Del Piero. Literally a legend. He's invited us over to LA to film with him. Del Piero! I can't put into words what that means to me.

Jez: But it happens so much. Cristiano Ronaldo said the same thing. He said his son loves our stuff and is watching our videos all the time.

It's a bittersweet experience, to be fair though. On the one hand it's a buzz to think that Ronaldo's son watches us but on the other, it makes us feel really old...

Billy: Ronaldo! It's just mad. Because when you create content you don't really think about these kind of people watching you. We think about the F2 fanbase – that's who we make it for.

It happened with Eden Hazard too. He came up to us before England played Belgium and said, 'my boys say you are their heroes and not me!'

He was joking around, pretending to be really angry about it. He was like, 'what's this about? I've got to be the hero!'

To be fair, I agree. Hazard should always be the hero!

Jez: Even the current crop of players, because we're getting a bit older and we've been doing it for 10 years, they grew up watching us. It's such a sweet spot. We've got all the tiers covered.

Billy: It's always exciting for us to meet top players. A lot of fans would love to be in that position, I know. But saying that, sometimes fans do get to meet big name players. That's always an exciting moment – but how can fans get the most out of it, Jez? What are the main dos and don'ts when you spot a football star out and about?

Jez: There's so much I can say. First, try to understand that these legends get stopped all the time. So, to you it might be just one picture you're asking for or just one moment of their time. But to the legend, that happens tonnes of times every day.

You can show them that you appreciate that you're taking some of their time. So you could say, 'Sorry for interrupting. Do you mind if I get a picture, if you've got time. It's okay if you haven't.'

Billy: Yeah, that alone will be hugely appreciated – that you've acknowledged you are taking up their time.

Jez: So don't assume they owe it to you and that the choice is theirs. There could be a million valid reasons why they don't want to interrupt their day for you.

Sometimes people don't show that they're appreciative. They just walk up to you with their phone, stick it in your face and just say, 'Picture' or 'Let me get a picture.'

Billy: Yeah, try and be better than that and you'll get better results.

Jez: If they're having family time, maybe dinner with their family, let them have that time. People think that just because you can see a legend in the flesh, it's an opportunity for a picture, autograph or conversation, but it's not necessarily.

Family time is precious. We only get a certain amount of time for living. Just because you can see them doesn't mean it's an opportunity. Try and gauge it. Leave it be sometimes.

Billy: All of which is a long way of saying that you should just show some basic manners. Meeting your heroes can be an amazing experience but you owe it to yourself to go about it respectfully and mindfully.

Jez: We've loved meeting legends like Gareth Bale. We hope you enjoy meeting some of your heroes, too!

BILLY

Heading: **Robert Lewandowski**
Mentality: **Cristiano Ronaldo**
Engine: **N'Golo Kanté**
Speed: **Kylian Mbappé**
Tekkers: **Neymar**
Passing: **Kevin De Bruyne**
Tackling: **Sergio Ramos**
Volleys: **Luis Suárez**
Dribbling: **Raheem Sterling**
Finishing: **Harry Kane**
Free Kicks: **Christian Eriksen**

JEZ

Heading: **Virgil Van Dijk**
Mentality: **Steven Gerrard**
Engine: **Tanguy Ndombele**
Speed: **Pierre-Emerick Aubameyang**
Tekkers: **Lionel Messi**
Passing: **Luka Modrić**
Tackling: **Giorgio Chiellini**
Volleys: **Zlatan Ibrahimović**
Dribbling: **Eden Hazard**
Finishing: **Sergio Agüero**
Free Kicks: **Paulo Dybala**

BUILD YOUR OWN FOOTBALLER ✏️

Okay guys, so you know our best player, now can you fill in yours? Will you agree with Billy, or will you side with Jez? Or will you disagree with both of us, and choose your own player for each category? That would be cheeky, but we won't take it too personally! Here's a reminder of our favourites and space for your own. Good luck!

Heading: vigil van Dijk

Mentality: cristiano ronaldo

Engine: N'golo Kante

Speed: H weng min soo

Tekkers: Lionel Messi

Passing: David silva

Tackling: John Terry

Volleys: Zlatan Ibbrohensovic

Dribbling: Isco

Finishing: Neymar Junior

Free Kicks: Giovani Locelso

OUTRO

So there we have it, guys. We really hope you enjoyed joining us as we put together the Ultimate Footballer. What a challenge. It's been emotional, right?

We're now proper deep into added time for this book but before we blow the final whistle and head for the dressing room we wanted to thank you for joining us and for supporting us over the years. F2 Family – we really appreciate you.

Which is why we also think it's important to remember the simple truth that runs throughout every attribute of the perfect player and which is also true for every star we have discussed in these pages.

The simple truth is that practice is what counts. Whether you're the best at dribbling, the fastest in your team or your side's greatest header, the truth is that you will have got there by practising.

Whether it's tackling, volleys or passing you want to perfect, you'll only improve by practice.

So don't think the elite players got where they are by some sort of magic. They might have been born with abilities but they got to the top by practising harder than anyone.

In reality, none of us can reach perfection because we're all human beings. Even Lionel Messi and Cristiano Ronaldo have a bad day sometimes. But what we can do is strive to be the best we can be – to reach our own personal peak. That's a reachable and beautiful target.

We can all work to get closer to perfection. Now you've read all about it, get out there and get working on upping your own game. We believe in you!

Love, peace and tekkers,

The F2

ACKNOWLEDGEMENTS

Now, this is the part where we usually thank our families, our publishers and the F2 staff. We know that without all of these guys, this book would not be possible, and we are so thankful for all their support in making this happen.

But we feel that, on book number five, we need to give all of our thanks to you – the reader and F2 Family member – who has enabled our hobbies to become our jobs, who will always be there to support us no matter what we are going through!

This is our fifth book, and the only reason why we have been able to do it is because of you and the support you give us. We will continue to do you proud and keep producing content and tekkers you love.

Thanks for being a massive part of our lives, and we can't wait to spend many more years with you.

Love, peace and tekkers,

Billy & Jezza

PHOTOGRAPHY CREDITS

The F2: 7 middle, 10, 13, 15, 29, 91, 92, 153, 154, 155, 167, 168, 169, 183, 185.

Dan Rouse: 6, 7, 16, 17, 18, 19, 24, 25, 27, 32, 33, 34, 35, 41, 42, 44, 45, 46, 47, 52, 53, 54, 55, 57, 59, 60, 61, 62, 63, 68, 69, 70, 71, 72, 73, 74, 75, 77, 78, 79, 80, 81, 86, 87, 88, 89, 94, 95, 96, 97, 102, 103, 104, 105, 107, 108, 109, 110, 111, 116, 117,118, 119, 120, 121, 122, 123, 125, 126, 127, 128, 129, 134, 135, 136, 137, 138, 139, 140, 141, 142, 142, 144, 145, 151, 156, 157, 158, 159, 165, 170, 171, 172, 173, 179, 180, 188.

Getty: 20, 21, 22, 23, 24 background, 30, 31, 36, 37, 38, 39, 48, 49, 50, 51, 52 background, 54 background, 64, 65, 66, 67, 82, 83, 84, 85, 86 background, 88 background, 89 bottom, 93, 98, 99, 100, 101, 102 background, 104 background, 113, 114, 115, 116 background, 118 background, 119 bottom, 120 background, 122 background, 130, 131, 132, 133, 134 background, 136 background, 138 background, 140 background, 146, 147, 148, 149, 160, 161, 162, 163, 174, 175, 176, 177, 186.